THE ROAD SOUTH

THE ROAD SOUTH

PERSONAL STORIES OF THE FREEDOM RIDERS

B. J. HOLLARS

THE UNIVERSITY OF ALABAMA PRESS   TUSCALOOSA

The University of Alabama Press
Tuscaloosa, Alabama 35487-0380
uapress.ua.edu

Typeface: Minion Pro

Cover image: Freedom Riders boarding a Trailways bus under heavy guard
by state troopers and National Guardsmen in Montgomery, Alabama, as
they prepare to leave for Mississippi, May 24, 1961; *New York World-Telegram
& Sun* Newspaper Photograph Collection, Library of Congress, Prints and
Photographs Division (LC-USZ62-135496)
Cover design: David Nees

Library of Congress Cataloging-in-Publication Data

Names: Hollars, B. J., author.
Title: The road south : personal stories of the Freedom Riders / B. J. Hollars.
Description: Tuscaloosa : The University of Alabama Press, [2018] | Includes
    bibliographical references and index.
Identifiers: LCCN 2017044600| ISBN 9780817319809 (cloth) | ISBN
    9780817391799 (ebook)
Subjects: LCSH: Freedom Rides, 1961—Personal narratives. | Civil rights
    workers—United States—Interviews. | Civil rights demonstrations—
    United States—History—20th century. | Civil rights demonstrations—
    Southern States—History—20th century. | Civil rights workers—United
    States—History—20th century. | African Americans—Segregation—
    Southern States—History—20th century. | Segregation in transportation—
    Southern States—History—20th century. | African Americans—Civil
    rights—Southern States—History—20th century. | Civil rights
    movements—Southern States—History—20th century. | Southern States—
    Race relations—History—20th century.
Classification: LCC E185.61 .H715 2018 | DDC 323.1196/073075—dc23
LC record available at https://lccn.loc.gov/2017044600

For Mom and Dad,
who would have told me to get on the bus.

And for the Riders—past, present, future.

The hope of our future lies in the fact that how change will come cannot be predicted. There is always the moment when the astonishing thing happens, when the changers abruptly leave the highway marked out for them and take to new, unmade paths. This is as it should be.

—Lillian Smith, in her introduction to James Peck's *Freedom Rides*

Contents

Figures

Acknowledgments

There are many to thank, and that's a good thing: it confirms that writing is never a solitary pursuit, even when it feels like one.

I am indebted to so many for so much. You probably know who you are, and I apologize in advance if, from brevity or forgetfulness, I have omitted your name here. Much like the Freedom Riders, you sought no credit, although you deserve it.

There are many whom I would like to thank by name, starting with the generous folks who opened up their homes and hearts throughout my road trip and beyond: D'Karlos Craig, Dr. John Fox, Paul Savides, Sarah and Patrick Connor, Dan and Jeanette Waterman, Dr. Valda Montgomery, Vera Harris, Arione Irby, Pete Conroy, Seyram Selase, Dr. Norman Golar, Michael Martone, Theresa Pappas, Jerry Mitchell, Dorothy Walker, Laura Anderson, Jim Alf, and Minnie Watson.

Thanks to my inspiring students, especially the spring 2016 participants in the civil rights pilgrimage.

A special thanks as well to my graduate student assistants: Joe Thunstrom, Monica Vargas, Jodie Arnold, and Samuel Hovda—all of whom helped me see what I couldn't see, opening my eyes through their own close readings.

Thank you to my colleagues and friends at the University of Wisconsin–Eau Claire as well: Chancellor James Schmidt, Provost Patricia Kleine, President Kimera Way, Dean David Leaman, Executive Director for Diversity and Inclusion Jodi Thesing-Ritter, Dean Carmen Manning, Chair Erica Benson, Dr. Audrey Fessler, Dr. David Jones, Jon Loomis, Allyson Loomis, Molly Patterson, Nick Butler, John Hildebrand, Max Garland, Bruce Taylor, Greg Kocken, Dr. Justin Patchin, Dr. Jason Spraitz, Dr. Paul Thomas, Dr.

James Rybicki, Dr. Jan Larson, Joanne Erickson, Olivia Vrunik, Steve Butler, and Scott Hub.

In addition, thank you to Dr. Karen Havholm and the Office of Research and Sponsored Programs at the University of Wisconsin–Eau Claire, whose University Research and Creative Activity grant proved vital to this project. Thanks too for the support provided by the University of Wisconsin–Eau Claire Academic Affairs Professional Development Program.

To the scholars who have done so much to ensure that the Freedom Riders are never forgotten: most notably Dr. Raymond Arsenault, Eric Etheridge, David Halberstam, Dr. Derek Catsam, and Stanley Nelson Jr. All of you have my sincere gratitude. Isaac Newton once noted that we "stand on the shoulders of giants." You are the giants.

A special thanks to the many archivists and special collections librarians who provided me much assistance, the Alabama Historical Commission for its support of the Freedom Riders Museum, and the Birmingham Civil Rights Institute.

To the University of Alabama Press, and in particular, Editor-in-Chief Dan Waterman, Assistant Managing Editor Joanna Jacobs, and copy editor Judith Antonelli. This book is infinitely better because of you.

To the Freedom Riders, and specifically the Riders included herein: James Zwerg, Susan (Wilbur) Wamsley, Miriam (Feingold) Real, Charles Person, Bernard LaFayette Jr., Bill Harbour, Catherine Burks-Brooks, Hezekiah Watkins, Ernest "Rip" Patton, Henry "Hank" Thomas, and the many others whom I had the pleasure of meeting during our shared time at the Freedom Rides Museum. Their inspiring stories are what drove me to dedicate a portion of my life to writing this book.

Special thanks also to the Freedom Riders who chatted with me before my trip: Carol Ruth Silver, Bob Zellner, Thomas Armstrong, David Fankhauser, Rick Sheviakov, Jerry Ivor Moore, and photographer Jim Peppler.

To the Wait! What Writers (we've got to come up with a better name) and, in particular, Ken Szymanski and Eric Rasmussen, both of whom read more than their fair share in service to this book.

And finally, to my family, which always boards the bus alongside me. Thanks for joining me on this beautiful ride.

Author's Note

When one is writing history, the stories are only as good as those who have preserved them. I am thankful that many scholars and archivists have done so much to preserve the story of the Freedom Riders.

While I relied heavily on the sources noted in the bibliography, the majority of this book's information is the result of personal interviews with the Freedom Riders. These conversations gave me access to the more personal moments of the movement, a goal that was always at the forefront of this project. I wanted to share with readers the moments that hadn't been shared before. In addition, I wanted to move beyond the "what happened when" questions and instead focus on the people themselves. As such, this work is not meant to be an all-encompassing historical text on the Freedom Rides; for that I refer you to Dr. Raymond Arsenault's *Freedom Riders* and Dr. Derek Catsam's *Freedom's Main Line*. Instead, I have attempted to tell the Riders' personal stories, to share their historic contributions by revealing what they hold in their hearts.

When possible, I fact-checked the details of each Freedom Rider's account, but in some instances the Riders' personal experiences transcended the typical fact-checking. How, after all, can one confirm what went through a man's mind as he was beaten unconscious on a street in Montgomery? And how can one know for certain what a young woman thought while trapped behind the bars at Parchman Farm?

I note this simply as an acknowledgment that the truth is often hard to pin down, particularly when it resides beyond the written record. To this end, what you have before you are the personal stories from the people who lived them. Although I was aware of the problems of bias and memory, when it came to these individuals' stories, I took the Riders at their word.

Then, assuming that the record didn't contradict their accounts, I wrote those words as best I could.

Words in quotation marks were taken from interviews or the published record. On occasion, an interviewee re-created dialogue for a scene based on his or her firsthand account, as Jim Zwerg did when describing his arrest by Bull Connor and his time in the Birmingham City Jail, when Jerry Mitchell recounted his interactions with Byron De La Beckwith, and when Hezekiah Watkins described his interactions with a police officer and James Bevel. Italicized phrases signify re-created thoughts or dialogue, based on primary and secondary sources.

THE ROAD SOUTH

Figure 1. James Farmer, mug shot, May 24, 1961.

Prologue

All Aboard

On the morning of Thursday, May 4, 1961, thirteen passengers—seven black and six white—purchased their bus tickets at the Trailways and Greyhound stations in Washington, DC, and prepared themselves for their journey. Leading the way was forty-one-year-old African American James Farmer, the newly appointed national director of the Congress of Racial Equality (CORE). Meticulously dressed in a suit and tie, Farmer ran his eyes over the silver buses that would soon transport him and his fellow Freedom Riders directly into the heart of Dixie. His formal attire was hardly a matter of style, but—like everything else—a calculation. Farmer demanded that every detail of their journey be planned, right down to the dress code. It was his way of maintaining control of the narrative, of proving to the American public that the Freedom Riders were hardly the commie-loving, rabble-rousing northerners they'd soon be pegged as, but only citizens demonstrating for their basic rights.

Although their Freedom Ride might not have been common knowledge to every American, certainly the primary stakeholders were informed. Farmer had personally seen to it—explaining the Riders' intentions in a flurry of letters sent to President John Kennedy, Attorney General Robert Kennedy, and the presidents and chairmen of the Greyhound and Trailways bus lines. He appealed directly to the media as well, and in late April 1961 he informed a *New York Post* reporter that the Freedom Riders were at last "ready to roll."

Despite this groundwork, the politicians, bus companies, and media seemed mostly uninterested in CORE's journey. It was hardly shaping up to be the media draw Farmer had hoped for. The press was busy that day: in just twenty-four hours astronaut Alan Shepard was scheduled to begin the trip that would earn him the title of the first American in space. In comparison, a few folks boarding buses to New Orleans hardly seemed worthy of newsprint. Yet their boarding was only the beginning of their story; the real drama wouldn't reveal itself for another ten days, when blood began to spill in the streets.

In retrospect the irony is unmistakable: we possessed the technology to launch a man into space yet lacked the humanity to share a bus seat. But as Farmer faced the modest crowd that day, there were other ironies to consider as well. Despite two Supreme Court decisions (1946's *Morgan v. Virginia* and 1960's *Boynton v. Virginia*) that had ruled against segregation in public or interstate transporation vehicles and facilities, several southern cities still dictated where black people were allowed to sit on interstate buses and where they were allowed to eat within the travel facilities themselves. Whereas the *Morgan* decision confirmed that a state's attempt to enforce segregation on interstate bus travel was in violation of the Interstate Commerce Clause, the *Boynton* decision went even further, confirming the illegality of segregated facilities within the bus terminals. Taken together, these rulings couldn't have been clearer: segregation should not happen on interstate buses or in their terminals.

Bus lines and facilities that ignored these rulings were therefore in direct violation of the Supreme Court. Yet, in many cases, custom trumped the court. In an effort to expose this problem, CORE began preparing for the Freedom Riders' journey. CORE believed it was essential for all Americans to understand the African American plight as well as the contempt some southerners felt toward the highest court in the land. If southerners wouldn't listen to the Supreme Court, CORE reasoned, perhaps they would listen to the court of public opinion. But first the organization had to find a way for the country to hear its case—develop some strategy to grab attention.

In his book *The Children*, David Halberstam confirmed that the 1955–1956 Montgomery Bus Boycott had indeed "touched a resonant nerve nationally." What remained unclear, however, was just how long that resonance might last. Post–bus boycott, the new role of the activist, Halberstam explained, was to "lure the beast of segregation to the surface and show to ordinary Americans just exactly how it was that the leadership of the South maintained . . . segregation." In doing so, the federal government would have no choice but to act—or so the activists hoped.

On the morning of May 4, 1961, the beast was baited again. Standing alongside the buses, James Farmer invoked a martyr's tone, informing the press—and by extension, its readers—that he and his fellow Freedom Riders were prepared to endure violence and, if arrested, would serve their sentences. "We will not pay fines," he declared in his baritone voice, "because we feel that by paying money to a segregated state we would help it perpetuate segregation."

The reporters scrawled Farmer's words onto their notepads and then, at the conclusion of his remarks, watched as the men and women dutifully took their seats on the buses. Fifty-five years later, while scrolling through the microfilmed news reports, I wonder: *What must the Freedom Rides have seemed like to those reporters?* A death wish? A crusade? Something in between? Did they roll their eyes? Sigh heavily? Whisper of the horrors sure to befall the Riders?

Although violence seemed likely, it was hardly guaranteed. In fact, as history had proven fourteen years earlier, integrated bus travel throughout the South could sometimes go unnoticed. In the spring of 1947 the Friendship of Reconciliation (FOR), the American Friends Service Committee (AFSC), and CORE had banded together to embark on a similar challenge, known as the Journey of Reconciliation: a meandering two-week bus trip to test the enforcement of the recently passed *Morgan v. Virginia* decision. The ruling had struck down racial segregation on interstate buses, but it hardly guaranteed local law enforcement's cooperation. The journey—undertaken by sixteen men, both black and white—had shuttled travelers throughout the upper South (Washington, DC, and Virginia, North Carolina, Tennessee, and Kentucky) with little violence. In fact, the lack of violence ultimately diminished their cause, reducing their trip to a nonstory.

The old dictum "If it bleeds, it leads" appeared to be true—or at least its inverse: without violence, a story is often forgotten. Certainly James Farmer understood the connection between violence and media coverage. And in an effort to receive coverage, he accepted the advice of CORE's inner circle to route its trip directly through the Deep South—Georgia, Alabama, Mississippi, and Louisiana—rather than flirt along the southern border states as the Journey of Reconciliation had done. In addition, Farmer agreed that the Freedom Riders shouldn't limit their tests solely to bus seating but should include bus terminals as well. In this way their nonviolent direct-action protest could simultaneously challenge enforcement of both the *Morgan* and *Boynton* rulings.

"I thought [the trip was] a capital idea," Farmer later remarked. "But it should not be called a Journey of Reconciliation. Such a name would be out of touch with the scrappy nonviolence movement that had emerged. The cry, I said, was not for 'reconciliation' but for '*freedom.*' It would be called the 'Freedom Ride.'"

———

Fifty-five years later I embarked on my own ride as a participant in my university's biannual civil rights pilgrimage: a twenty-seven-hundred-mile bus trip from Wisconsin throughout the South. Our mission was to see, feel, and experience as much of the American civil rights movement as can be squeezed into nine days. It's a daunting journey, and about a hundred students sign up for each trip. I was well aware of the trip's reputation for leaving its participants emotionally exhausted and forever changed. For years I had witnessed students return from this trip transformed. It was as if their worlds were suddenly widened.

Although I had spent four years studying and teaching at the University of Alabama before moving to Wisconsin, my own world still required some widening. I too yearned for this transformation, and even though I was less than thrilled by the requisite exhaustion that accompanied it, that was a price I was willing to pay. And it was a small price: I faced no mobs, no bombs, no beatings. Who was I to complain about a crick in my neck?

Our eyes were opened in Atlanta, Birmingham, and Montgomery and then opened further in Selma, New Orleans, and Little Rock. They were opened so much, in fact, that after a while we couldn't shut them even when we tried. Suddenly injustice was everywhere, and not just in the past. "Too much information," one student repeated wearily after our museum visits, our plantation tour, our slavery reenactment, and our many conversations on the bus.

He was right; it was too much information. And neither of us knew how to bear it.

Shortly after my stint with the students on the bus, I planned a second ride: a solo expedition aimed at meeting the original Freedom Riders who had boarded the buses fifty-five years ago. Although many of the Freedom Riders have since died, many still remain—living history for those who seek them. After making countless phone calls and sending numerous emails, I began to wear many of them down. They had told their stories several times before, but I begged them for one more retelling. "All right," one Freedom

Rider after another agreed, which was often followed by "You're pretty persistent, you know that?"

I unfurled a map and, based on their locations, began plotting my own ride—not that there were any facilities left for me to test. For a white heterosexual man of the modern era like me, there's hardly a place on the planet where privilege doesn't pave my way. Thus my ride was never about testing facilities or the enforcement of laws, as it was for the Freedom Riders. Instead I hoped to gather the stories from the Riders themselves, the people who made the choice to risk their lives by boarding a bus—and bucking custom—right here in the United States.

Although much has been written on the Freedom Rides, far less has been written on the Riders themselves. Scholarship often includes brief biographical sketches of who they were, but I've often wondered: Who were they *really*? And where are they now?

The answer to the first question is that they were men and women from all walks of life—black and white, young and old, northerner and southerner—but mostly, as a 1962 survey conducted by Johns Hopkins University confirmed, they were educated young people. Although recent scholarship notes a nearly equal proportion of black and white participants, the Johns Hopkins survey claimed that 63 percent of Freedom Riders were white and 36 percent were black. Moreover, it recorded that 55 percent of Freedom Rider respondents were male and 43 percent were female. Finally, 74 percent of the white Riders were college graduates, and an additional 22 percent had attended "some college." This was in contrast to 47 percent of black Riders who had college degrees and 34 percent noting "some college." (These numbers were from a Johns Hopkins study in the CORE files that did not provide any information on which of the Freedom Riders who claimed "some college" later went on to complete their degrees. Since many Riders were enrolled college students, presumably most did finish their college educations after participating in the Freedom Rides.)

This demographic information confirmed what I thought I knew of the Freedom Riders. Part of the power of their story, after all, is a result of their diversity. That black and white people risked their lives in common cause served only to strengthen their cause. Yet this information did little to answer my second question: Where are they now?

Ultimately, this question led to the way I have organized this book. Rather than giving a chronological historical retelling, I've instead attempted to answer the "Where are they now?" question by dedicating each chapter to an individual and primarily ordering the chapters based on the chronology of the interviews. In doing so, I hope to delve deeper into the interior experiences of the people who risked their lives in pursuit of social justice while also revealing my own greater understanding of the Freedom Rides as my journey progressed. On occasion the Freedom Riders' stories overlap, providing new vantage points for scenes with which the reader is already familiar. Yet this overlap is important to the larger story: a confirmation that the messiness of history never yields to a single narrative.

There are problems, however, with this organization: one chapter per Rider can provide no more than a glimpse of a life. In writing the screenplay for the 1982 film *Gandhi*, John Briley faced a similar challenge: How can a writer ever encapsulate the entirety of a life on the page? "No man's life can be encompassed in one telling," he conceded. "There is no way to give each year its allotted weight, to include each event, each person who helped to shape a lifetime." Instead, he argued, the best a writer can do is to be "faithful in spirit to the record and to try to find one's way to the heart of the man."

With these words in mind, I have come to feel that I know the hearts of many Freedom Riders through the stories they shared. I don't attempt to tell their entire life stories, only the story of their lives. For eight months or so my phone was constantly at my ear as I listened to their stories. But every time I hung up, I couldn't help but feel as if I had just begun to understand their plights. What I was missing, I realized, was firsthand experience, the chance to wear down some tire tread myself.

So in May 2016, fifty-five years after the Freedom Rides, I hung up the phone and headed for the car. There were places I needed to see, people I needed to meet, and lessons I needed to learn. And who better to teach me than the Freedom Riders themselves?

I buckled up, put my foot on the accelerator, and let the road lead me south.

PART I

The Road Behind

Figure 2. James Zwerg, yearbook photo, 1962.

Used by permission of Beloit College Archives.

1

James Zwerg

Appleton, Wisconsin

*"We're dedicated to this. We'll take hitting, we'll take
beating. We're willing to accept death."*

In the fall of 1958, eighteen-year-old James Zwerg—Jim, to his friends—set
foot on Beloit College's Wisconsin campus for his first day of classes. A
native of Appleton, Jim was anxious to find his future somewhere among
the white-columned red-brick buildings that speckled the tree-lined quad.
The tall, lean Wisconsinite had dreams of earning a sociology degree and,
having come from a supportive middle-class family, seemed poised to do
so—or to do anything else he wanted, for that matter. For the moment, the
world was his for the taking, and everything was going as planned.

With bags in tow, Jim entered Haven Hall and scanned the narrow cor-
ridors in search of his dorm room. He had been assigned not one roommate
but two—doubling his odds of making friends, he figured. Upon entering
the room, he soon locked eyes with one of his roommates, a black student
named Bob Carter.

Jim was momentarily taken aback. He was not upset, only surprised.
Having grown up in Appleton, Jim's firsthand experiences with black people were limited. "All through high school," Jim told me in a phone interview, "I didn't know anyone with a different ethnic background."

Nevertheless, the pair became fast friends, and they could often be spotted
roaming the quad together on the way to the commons or to class. The more
time they spent together in public, the more Jim became acutely aware of
both overt and covert instances of racial prejudice. "We'd go to the commons
to have a meal, and people would get up from the table to leave," Jim recalled.
"And there were these excessive tiffs during basketball or football intramural
games. People made comments just loud enough for [Bob] to hear."

One afternoon Jim invited Bob to visit the fraternity he had recently pledged, only to learn when Bob stepped inside that their so-called brotherhood hardly extended to black men. His "brothers" made it clear that Bob was not welcome in the house. For Jim, this was the first of many moral crises to come, but this particular one was easily resolved. Jim returned his fraternity pin, preferring to find true brotherhood elsewhere.

Throughout his freshman year, Jim observed instances of discrimination in the city as well, including one situation in which a barber refused Bob service because he didn't cut "Negro" hair. Jim was puzzled by such overt instances of racism, but he was even more puzzled by Bob's muted response. "How do you take it?" Jim asked one day while the pair lounged in their dorm room. "Why don't you do something?"

Bob's eyes flickered toward Jim, and after a moment of contemplation he walked over to his dresser. Removing a copy of Dr. Martin Luther King's *Stride toward Freedom*, he encouraged his roommate to read it. Jim opened the book, and what he found inside proved life-changing. The book lays out the strategy that Dr. King employed throughout the 1955–1956 Montgomery Bus Boycott—the thirteen-month demonstration that led to a federal ruling and a Supreme Court decision that confirmed the unconstitutionality of segregated buses. Yet Dr. King's book was more than a mere blueprint; it described not only the movement's overall strategy but its nonviolent philosophical underpinnings as well.

"I could understand the boycotts," Jim told me, "but this nonviolence business, I didn't really get a good handle on it at that point." Yet Jim soon realized that Dr. King's nonviolence strategy—which King credited to Mahatma Gandhi—was deeply rooted in his own Christian faith. Nonviolence was about "turning the other cheek," Jim explained to me; it was about rendering one's persecutors powerless by refusing to fight back. The strategy, Jim decided, was either ingenious or ludicrous; he would soon find out which for himself.

======

In the early part of 2016, just a few months after talking with Jim, I wandered through the library book sale in my hometown of Eau Claire, Wisconsin, and stumbled upon a 1958 edition of *Stride toward Freedom*. It was a gift from the universe, I was certain—akin to Bob Carter handing his copy to Jim. I flipped through the book's brittle pages and imagined Jim doing the same all those years before. I couldn't help but search for traces of Jim in its pages, homing in on sections that I imagined might drive a young white college student to act.

I found one such trace in a chapter titled "Where Do We Go from Here?" In it Dr. King noted that Montgomery's racial problems were but a microcosm of the country's wider problems with race. As such, the title's question had national implications. The answer to Dr. King's question, which soon become evident to the leadership team of CORE, was that demonstrators must go to the South. And in doing so, they could utilize buses in a way other than just as their means of transportation: not by boycotting them, as had been done in Montgomery, but by boarding them instead. While Dr. King rightfully credited the Montgomery Bus Boycott as a formative moment for black southerners, he also understood the boycott's effects on white America: a segment of white citizens was at last taking note of the problems of segregation. Jim Zwerg was among them.

In the fall of 1960 Jim was accepted into an exchange program between Beloit College and Fisk University, a historically black university in Nashville, Tennessee—an opportunity that provided a front-row seat to the burgeoning civil rights movement. Yet it also provided the mild-mannered Wisconsinite the chance to participate himself, an opportunity he soon took advantage of.

Upon his arrival in Nashville in January 1961, Jim became enamored of Fisk. The university was a hotbed of ideas, a living laboratory where young black students seemed compelled to take their classroom lessons and apply them to life. It was a departure from his experiences at Beloit, not only demographically but also in terms of the students' objectives. At Fisk, Jim observed, the students seemed both intellectually *and* morally engaged, and he marveled at their brazen willingness to occasionally overlook the former for the latter. Fisk students recognized the importance of studying history, but they also recognized the importance of making it. Of course, there was a third option, too: study history *while* making it—which was precisely what many students did throughout the spring of 1960 as they took their seats at Nashville's lunch counters.

As a result of the highly successful lunch-counter sit-ins, Nashville soon solidified its reputation as a battleground for civil rights. Fisk University, along with institutions such as the American Baptist Theological Seminary and Tennessee Agricultural and Industrial State College (now known as

Tennessee State University), earned a reputation for churning out socially conscious students—many of whom became leaders in the Nashville movement and beyond.

Chief among them was a twenty-two-year-old Fisk University English major named Diane Nash, whose intellect and courage soon propelled her to the forefront of Nashville's civil rights scene. The previous spring Nash had attended a conference at Shaw University in Atlanta, where she, along with many other students, helped form the Student Nonviolent Coordinating Committee (SNCC), which would play a role in a number of civil rights actions, from the Freedom Rides to the 1963 March on Washington to 1964's Freedom Summer.

Nash, a native of Chicago, had begun her college career at Howard University in Washington, DC, before transferring to Fisk in the fall of 1959. Upon her arrival in the Upper South, she soon gained a new appreciation for the challenges of segregation, and she committed herself to helping to overcome those challenges. In addition to possessing great intellect and courage, Nash was a force in front of the television cameras—a savvy and well-spoken student who was keenly aware of the importance of messaging in a media-driven world. A light-skinned black woman with green eyes, she was considered photogenic as well and was even a former beauty pageant runner-up; her electricity further helped her hold an audience. For years Nash's innumerable strengths served the movement well—from her regional work integrating Nashville's lunch counters and movie theaters to her responsibilities overseeing a portion of the Freedom Rides soon to come.

For Jim Zwerg, Nash was nothing short of inspiring—a fellow northerner whose stoic, clear-eyed vision appeared unshakable. He hoped that he would develop similarly, although upon his arrival in Nashville it was evident that he still had a long way to go. Back in Beloit Jim had wondered what it might be like to be in the minority, and when he entered the Fisk student union one day in January 1961, his question was no longer hypothetical. Not only was he in the minority, but his sandy blond hair and six-foot-tall frame ensured that he'd have a hard time blending in. When a black couple spotted the white student peering bleary-eyed at the bustling student union, they invited him to their table. Jim gratefully accepted, and the trio dedicated the afternoon to casual chitchat, picking at french fries, and watching as their fellow students crowded the dance floor. "What's that?" Jim asked, curious about the dance moves flashing before them.

"The twist," the couple informed him.

"Oh, I know the twist," Jim said confidently, but when he set out to prove it on the dance floor, he soon learned that his knowledge was limited to the "Wisconsin twist"—a variation that was, as he put it, "very flat-footed" compared to the loose jive being performed by the Fisk students.

What Jim lacked in twisting skills he soon made up for with his congenial nature. He was quick to befriend the couple, and in an effort to continue the fun as the afternoon wound down, suggested they take in a movie together. The couple stared at him in disbelief. "Jim," one of his new friends said, "we *can't* take in a movie together. The movie theaters in Nashville are segregated."

The Wisconsinite could hardly believe it. "That's the dumbest thing I ever heard," he said. "Who are they to say who I can and can't go to a movie with?"

The two black students looked at each other, then told Jim that if he was serious about integrating Nashville's theaters—*really* serious—he was welcome to join a newly formed effort committed to doing so. Jim was intrigued, and within days he situated himself across the street from a Nashville movie theater to witness a demonstration in progress.

"There was a group, maybe a dozen [people], just standing there in front of the movie theater," he told me. "All were nicely dressed. The guys were all in suits and ties, and the girls were all in dresses. But they just stood there. They didn't have placards, they weren't singing any freedom songs, they weren't trying to get any tickets. They just stood there."

Curious about the demonstrators' reserved demeanor, Jim crossed the street and struck up a conversation with the last person in line. "I've been watching you," he said. "What is it you're trying to accomplish?"

"You need to speak to our spokesman," the demonstrator said, nodding toward a young black man ahead of them.

"So I went to that gentleman," Jim told me, "and that was John Lewis."

The John Lewis: a man whose humble origins as the son of sharecroppers in Troy, Alabama, hardly prevented him from becoming one of the most storied leaders of the civil rights movement; a man destined to be a Freedom Rider, a marcher from Selma to Montgomery, a Freedom Summer volunteer, and a chairman of SNCC; a man whose service to his country continues to this day as the congressman for Georgia's fifth district.

Lewis eyed the curious white student towering above him, deemed him sincere, and invited Jim to join him and the others back at the church after the demonstration. Jim agreed, and as a result of that initial meeting—in which he first witnessed the raw, unstoppable power of young people bonded in common cause—he soon became a regular among the activists. Yet even then Jim wasn't fully committed to accepting nonviolence in his life. Despite having been inundated with various testimonies and Bible verses on the subject, Jim still couldn't wrap his head around the idea of purposely allowing oneself to be vulnerable. "I wrestled with those testimonies," Jim told me. "The Sermon on the Mount was a big one."

In fact, "an eye for an eye" made logical sense to twenty-one-year-old Jim, whereas "turn the other cheek" seemed far more useful in theory than in practice. But one night, after spending time with black students from the American Baptist Theological Seminary, Jim was struck by the power of nonviolence in both theory *and* practice. "It just hit me one evening that the gospels—the story of Jesus—were the most powerful story of nonviolent direct action ever written. 'My God,' I thought. 'That's what it means to be a Christian.'"

Jim was anxious to throw himself headlong into the demonstrations, but first he needed to undergo the Nashville Student Movement's nonviolence training sessions, many of which involved role-playing. As Jim soon learned, his skin color made him uniquely qualified for one role in particular: the white bigot. Jim, who had joined the movement in an effort to combat racism, soon found himself slinging the very words he would never have dreamed of saying under other circumstances.

"I used words that my Mama would have washed my mouth out for," Jim admitted. As uncomfortable as it was, he knew it was all for the cause. Nevertheless, he looked forward to the day when his participation in the movement would transcend role-playing, when he could use his privilege as a target rather than a shield.

He got his chance weeks later when he took his place in a movie theater ticket line with his fellow demonstrators. To the ticket seller in the booth, his exterior surely pegged him as the perfect patron: clean-cut, well-dressed, and, as his skin color confirmed, certainly not one of those black agitators who had so forcefully integrated lunch counters in the past year. Indeed, he resembled just another white moviegoer, his outward appearance offering no hint of the convictions the young man held in his heart—or the fact that he intended to buy tickets not only to use himself but to hand out to black demonstrators as well.

Eventually Jim made his way to the front of the line and purchased a pair of tickets without incident. Then he did so again at a nearby theater, and another, going to four nearby movie theaters until a few of the managers grew wise to the ruse and refused to sell the white man any more tickets to distribute to his rabble-rousing friends.

Jim rejoined his fellow demonstrators back at one of the theaters, handing a ticket to Bill Harbour, his partner in testing the establishment. Armed only with their nonviolence training, Jim and Bill strode toward the doors. Although the men tried hard to hide their fear, they surely felt it. After all, they were preparing to undertake a dangerous mission, violating both custom and law to combat segregation. "We got inside the doors," Jim explained. "Then we were both coldcocked and dumped out on the sidewalks."

"And that," he told me, "was my introduction to being a demonstrator."

=====

Jim could hardly have known it at the time, but his assault at the movie theater was just a glimpse of the violence soon to befall him. Throughout much of the spring the Nashville Student Movement remained focused on integrating the theaters, and by mid-May it at last found success.

On Sunday, May 14—Mother's Day—the group had organized a celebratory picnic, but the celebration was cut short when the students received news of the tragic fate of the interstate bus trip known as the Freedom Rides. For the Nashville students, the details remained hazy, but the generalities were clear: ten days into the journey, CORE's effort to take buses throughout the South had ended in violence. One bus was set aflame outside Anniston, Alabama, and soon after the Riders on the second bus were beaten in Birmingham's Trailways bus terminal.

The picnickers headed to their nearby office, where they immediately began strategizing a response. For the past week and a half the students had closely followed the news of the Riders, supporting their brethren from afar. Yet upon learning of the violence that had befallen them, it was now clear to Nash and the other student leaders that their good wishes were not enough.

When word reached them that Farmer was planning to halt CORE's journey as a result of the violence, the Nashville students committed themselves to continuing where the others left off. They believed they had no choice. Halting the Rides, the students feared, would only teach the segregationists that their violence was effective. Nash placed calls to Farmer and Dr. King, informing them of the Nashville students' intentions. Both men urged her to reconsider, but she remained undeterred.

When the White House heard about the students' plan, Attorney General Robert Kennedy placed a call to John Seigenthaler, the thirty-three-year-old award-winning former reporter for the *Tennessean* and one of the few southerners in the Justice Department.

It was two o'clock in the morning, but the attorney general didn't think twice about waking his special assistant. *You know Diane Nash?* Kennedy demanded. Seigenthaler agreed that he knew her, though not half as well as a friend of his, a Nashville-based attorney named George Barrett, did. The attorney general informed Seigenthaler that somebody needed to persuade Nash to halt the Freedom Rides, and Seigenthaler assured Kennedy that Barrett would relay that message directly. Soon after doing so, however, Barrett learned that the request had fallen on deaf ears.

The students were going, Barrett informed Seigenthaler in a follow-up phone call. Not even a request from the attorney general would dissuade them. Furious, Seigenthaler punched Nash's number on the telephone keypad and spoke directly to the twenty-two-year-old woman. "You know, you're sending people to their death," he informed her bluntly.

Nash replied that she was aware of the risks—they all were—and that the Riders had already made out their wills.

———

Despite the grave misgivings of both the civil rights leaders and the federal government, on the morning of Wednesday, May 17, 1961, Jim Zwerg and several others bought their bus tickets to Birmingham. Since more than enough Riders had volunteered for the journey, it was up to the Nashville Student Movement leaders to decide which ones were most prepared for the challenges that lay ahead.

Jim was humbled to have been selected; perhaps he was chosen not only for his preparedness but also because of the demographic he represented: a white man in active support of civil rights. It was a perilous position to fill, all but guaranteeing that the mobs would single him out. "When violence occurred, it followed a format," Jim explained to me. "And I was usually the first focus. They wanted the white [man]. I was the traitor of the white race."

Perhaps he was a traitor to some, but to others, such as President Kennedy, Jim was living proof of the ideal the president would promulgate during his civil rights address two years later that "the rights of every man are diminished when the rights of one man are threatened." Jim felt diminished each time his black friends were denied service at a lunch counter, at a movie theater, or at a particular place on a bus. And he had felt diminished when his former roommate, Bob Carter, was denied access to a fraternity house, a barber's chair, and a fair shake on the basketball court. This continual diminishment was simply too much for him to bear, which was why, late on the evening of May 16—just hours before boarding the bus—Jim reached for his pen and paper. "We were encouraged to write this little note or letter or whatever you want to call it—a last will and testament somebody called it—and Diane would hold them in the event that we were killed," Jim told me, confirming Seigenthaler's version. Although he couldn't recall exactly what he wrote that night, he remembered the gist: detailing to his parents his reasons for risking his life for others' freedom.

As he explained it, his decision to ride was a direct result of his upbringing. Born into a devout, progressive family, the Zwergs were known throughout the Appleton community as good, God-fearing people. Jim, in particular, had warmed to the Christian teachings he received each Sunday, and by high school he had sung in the church choir, served as an acolyte, and become the president of his youth group. Indeed, the seeds for his future pastoral work were already planted, and throughout his civil rights experiences, those seeds would continue to grow.

Even though Jim's father actively helped Appleton's low-income population by providing free dental work once a month, he was less than thrilled by his youngest son's involvement in the civil rights movement. It was one thing to fill a cavity at no charge but quite another for a white northerner to risk his life for a seat at a lunch counter, in a movie theater, or on a bus.

Jim had been discreet about his civil rights work, but he knew he could hardly join the Freedom Rides without informing his parents of his decision. Dropping his pen, he reached for the phone instead. "I wanted to tell them how much I loved them," he explained to me, "and to thank them for bringing me up the way they did." He paused, and I waited intently. "I guess I was naively hoping that I would get the kind of send-off that the young soldier gets: 'We're proud of you son. God bless you, keep safe.' And I didn't get that."

What he got instead was an earful from his mother. He'd hardly finished announcing his impending travel when Mary Zwerg interrupted. "You can't do that," she told him. "You're throwing away your education. Think of the money we spent."

Oh my God, Jim thought, *all you care about is the money?*

"And do you know what you'll do to your father?" she continued. "He can't take this, you can't do this to him." She knew it was her trump card, the only argument with the potential to give her son pause. His father had recently survived a heart attack, so Jim was well aware of his father's waning health. Yet he was also aware of the sickness of segregation that had spread throughout the country.

It pained him to be at odds with his parents, yet he saw no other choice. They'd raised him to combat injustice, which is precisely what he intended to do. "Mom," Jim stated, "I've never been so sure. This is what God wants me to do."

"You'll *kill* your father!" she exclaimed, slamming the phone into its cradle.

Jim returned to his dorm room, reached for his Bible, and sought solace in Psalm 27—his preferred passage during dark times. "The Lord is my light and my salvation—whom shall I fear? . . . Though a host should encamp against me, my heart shall not fear." Just a few lines down, Jim glanced at a verse even more fitting, given the circumstances: "Though my father and mother forsake me, the Lord will receive me."

"I read that over so many times," Jim said. "It was very, very hard for me. I didn't sleep very much that night. But I was *never* so certain in my entire life that what I was doing was God's will at that time."

=====

By the end of their first day as Freedom Riders, Jim and his seatmate, an African American man named Paul Brooks, found themselves behind bars in the Birmingham City Jail. Their bus had successfully traveled two hundred miles, but upon their arrival in Birmingham, Eugene "Bull" Connor, the city's notoriously violent commissioner of public safety, immediately put a halt to what he viewed as a flagrant disregard for state law.

As the bus shuddered to a stop, the door flung wide open, and on walked Connor himself. He eyed the Riders from behind his wire-rimmed glasses, then turned his attention to the driver.

"Y'all got some Freedom Riders from Nashville on here?" The driver nodded. "Can you point them out to me?" The driver turned, then pointed directly toward Jim and Paul Brooks just one seat back. Connor turned his attention to the Riders. "Come on, boy," Connor said to Paul Brooks. "You know you shouldn't be sitting there. Y'all get out of there now, come on."

From his seat by the window, Brooks explained that according to the *Morgan v. Virginia* Supreme Court ruling, it was illegal to segregate interstate buses. Furthermore, he added, he was quite comfortable in his current seat.

"All right, boy, you're under arrest," Connor said matter-of-factly. He told Jim to move out of the way, but Jim responded by echoing his seat-mate's remarks. A frustrated Connor sent both men to jail, where Jim and Paul Brooks spent the next two days.

Meanwhile, the rest of the Freedom Riders were soon to be trapped in the Birmingham bus terminal—a situation only slightly better than jail. As the Riders awaited a bus driver to take them to Montgomery, Jim found himself in the awkward position of being stone sober and trapped in the jail's drunk tank. There, amid forty or so white folks, Jim tried his best to blend in, or at least not be exposed as a civil rights–supporting northerner. Soon, however, his cover was blown.

"Hey," a man hollered, "this is one of them goddamned nigger-loving Freedom Riders."

Jim braced himself for the worst, but the worst did not befall him that day. The men gave him a hard time ("What the hell are you doing, boy? What's the matter with you?"), but for whatever reason, they stopped short of violence.

As the hours passed, Jim began earning the men's trust. Although they didn't have much in common, they shared an equal disgust for their deplorable living conditions in the tank. The floor was covered with vomit and feces, creating an odor so foul that even breathing became a challenge. After obtaining a few mops, Jim began organizing a cleanup crew, and as the men worked together to improve their shared space, they began to converse as well. And then, unexpectedly, they began to sing—a freedom song, no less. Jim started them off, and soon the others joined in: "Paul and Silas bound in jail / Got nobody to go on bail / Keep your eyes on the prize / Hold on."

When he was released from the tank two and a half days later, Jim was approached by a few of the men who still remained. "We don't necessarily agree with you," they said, shaking his hand, "but we think we understand why you're doing it."

Jim nodded. It was a start.

═══════

On the morning of May 20, Jim reunited with his fellow Riders at the Birmingham bus station. After much negotiation, the Kennedy administration had struck a deal with Alabama governor John Patterson, who agreed to protect the Freedom Riders during the remainder of their time in the state. As a result, that morning the Riders received an unprecedented escort as they journeyed deeper into Dixie.

"We had a plane going overhead," Jim recalled. "We had squad cars, we had motorcycles." Yet despite these momentary protections, their escort mysteriously turned away just as they entered Montgomery city limits. Suddenly the Freedom Riders were exposed, and they knew it. Jim turned to his seatmate, John Lewis, to find the future congressman just waking from his nap. Lewis watched as the last patrol car pulled out of sight, then said, "That's not good."

The bus eased into Montgomery's Greyhound station on South Court Street at around 10:20 A.M., and even though they feared for their lives, the Freedom Riders had no choice but to disembark. Jim followed the others, then huddled close around the press conference's microphones, uncertain of what was to come.

"John was just stepping forward to address the press," Jim said, "and this fella—I think he was a used car salesman, as I recall, and a Klansmen—went at one of the [reporters] . . . grabbed [that reporter's parabolic microphone], and threw it to the ground."

It was the spark that lit the fire, spurring a mob of about two hundred to emerge from all sides of the station, shove the press out of the way, and close in on the Freedom Riders. The following day's edition of the *Anniston Star* described the "howling mobs of white people" that raged for two hours, the women who attacked other women with purses, and the men who attacked the man who tried to stop it. Jim was in the midst of the mob, watching in horror as men came bearing bricks, pipes, and chains—all of which they used indiscriminately.

Meanwhile, from his perch a few floors up at a nearby federal building, John Doar, the US Assistant Attorney General for Civil Rights, watched on in horror. Doar, who had been dispatched to Montgomery to serve as the eyes and ears for the Justice Department, relayed a play-by-play back to Washington. "Oh, there are fists, punching!" he cried into the receiver. "There are no cops! It's terrible! It's terrible! There's not a cop in sight. People are yelling, 'There those niggers are! Get 'em, get 'em!' It's awful."

Unquestionably it was, though more so for the men and women left unprotected in the streets. As the mob swarmed toward him, Jim steeled himself and relied on his faith. Closing his eyes, he prayed to God for the strength to remain nonviolent in the midst of mortal danger. But he also prayed for the men who wielded those bricks, pipes, and chains, pleading with God to forgive them. "And that's when I had this incredible religious experience of feeling surrounded by love and peace," Jim told me, his voice quavering. "I just had this assurance that no matter what happened I was going to be okay."

In the moments after the beating, once Jim regained semiconsciousness, a photographer snapped a photo of the bloodied and beaten college student leaning against the edge of a building: his striped tie was slightly askew, despite his tie clip. With eyes lowered, he studied the blood on his sleeve as if wondering how it appeared there. But there was no question: the mob was to blame, even though there's no hint of its presence in the photo.

The following day, the bloodied photo of Jim made the front page of the *Montgomery Advertiser*, forcing white Alabamians to confront a bloodied face that resembled their own. The photograph graced newspapers across the country, yet for years Jim's neighbors and friends remained unaware of the dramatic role he had played in integrating interstate bus travel.

To some extent, Jim's anonymity was of his own making. His infamous photograph had made him a reluctant icon of a movement much larger than he. It was a role that made him uncomfortable, although the photo served a vital purpose: rousing white moderates from their passivity and demanding their own reckoning with race.

At some point during the beating Jim was knocked to the ground and pummeled further, and then he lost consciousness. He reawakened in St. Jude's Hospital, where he remained confined to his bed for five days; he has few memories of his time there, probably because he was unconscious for half of it. Yet memories from the morning of May 20 continue to come back in flashes: John Lewis handing him a handkerchief to wipe away the blood; the snarl of southern voices.

In the midst of this delirium, a second photographer snapped a photo of the now-famous Freedom Rider in his hospital bed. It shows a copy of the previous day's edition of the *Montgomery Advertiser* tucked neatly beneath his arm. The juxtaposition of the newspaper photo with the hospital bed photo managed to capture two versions of Jim Zwerg: one bloodied and one bruised, but both seemingly unmoved in their commitment to the cause.

His commitment was reaffirmed during a hospital bed interview recorded soon after the attack. In the footage, a black-eyed Jim can be heard saying, "We're dedicated to this. We'll take hitting, we'll take beating." And then, as his half-closed eyes fluttered toward the camera, Jim delivered his most powerful line: "We're willing to accept death."

In that moment his words held great weight—they were a signal to his fellow Riders, as well as to the nation, that violence would never deter them.

Yet years later Jim admitted to me that he hardly remembered any of it. He'd been fading in and out of consciousness throughout the interview, and when prompted to speak, he had simply repeated what he'd so often heard before, words that had become the mantra of the movement: that there was no turning back, not ever.

===

In addition to the physical violence, Jim paid an emotional toll. "A lot of the kids were disowned by their parents, were not welcomed back home," Jim explained years later. "I wasn't the only one who went through that." Even though he was in good company, this hardly made up for his fractured relationship with his family. "It was incredibly disappointing to me," he recalled, "that the people I loved the most didn't approve of what I'd done. Dad did have a little heart attack, and my mom had a bit of a breakdown, so I felt bad about that."

Although Jim recognized the strain he had placed on his family, he never predicted the lengths they would go to in refusing to support him in his fight for equality. On the evening of May 20, in the hours after her son's brutal beating in Montgomery, Mary Zwerg sat in her Appleton home on South Riverview Lane and reached for her personal stationery. In her careful script, she composed a passionate letter to Attorney General Kennedy, describing her son's plight and asking for information. "We are in great sympathy with the humanitarian goals of any effort toward racial justice," she affirmed, "but we are also aware that a group of highly idealistic and zealous students might easily be duped into subversive attitudes."

Although the line was written from a place of genuine concern, I can't imagine it sitting well with Jim. After all, he had hardly been "duped"; rather, his desire to be an agent for change was the result of much deep and soulful reflection. His transition from modest midwesterner to civil rights activist was the culmination of what he had seen, heard, and experienced throughout his college years. Furthermore, it was grounded in his religious beliefs. Although Jim's parents shared these beliefs, they didn't share their son's enthusiasm for putting them into practice in such a public and dangerous way.

"If you can give us any information or can suggest any counseling for our son which may channel his energies into the best use to his country and himself," Zwerg closed her letter, "his anxious parents will be most grateful."

A few months after my interview with Jim, I parked the car and slipped into the First Congregational United Church of Christ in my town of Eau Claire, Wisconsin. The church, as I had recently learned, was once home to Jim Zwerg. In fact, he served as its associate pastor from 1967 to 1971—long before my time, but recent enough that he is well-remembered by many of the faithful congregants who continue to fill the pews. One of them agreed to meet with me.

I took a seat in the church library and was joined by sixty-four-year-old Paul Savides, who had been a member of the youth group during Jim's time as associate pastor. "Hey, B. J.," Paul greeted me, removing his fedora and settling into the chair alongside my own. "It's nice to finally meet you."

We had previously conversed via email, but despite my attendance at this church for the past several months, we had not yet formally met. I shook his hand and thanked him for his time. "So tell me about Jim," I said.

"Well, the first time I met him was when he came to our house on Keith Street," Paul began. "He drove up—this big, tall guy, full of life energy just radiating—and it was just so attractive to me." He had no way of knowing it at the time, but on that summer day in 1967 Paul was standing face-to-face with the man who would long inspire his own commitment to social justice. Jim made no mention of his Freedom Ride during that initial meeting. Instead, Paul admired him simply for being the charismatic new youth group leader. As president of the youth group, Paul knew Jim would be a perfect fit.

Of the many interactions that followed, the experience Paul remembers most involved Jim organizing a youth group trip to Milwaukee during the summer of 1968—just a year after the city's national headline–grabbing riots. On July 30, 1967, racial tensions had reached a fever pitch, prompting black citizens to riot in protest of police brutality and housing discrimination. The riots continued for four days and resulted in four deaths, fifteen hundred arrests, and incalculable damage to the downtown area.

Jim was aware of the racial tensions in his home state, and in an effort to ensure that his youth group members were equally informed, he had organized a trip to the city. "I think the idea was for Jim to give us some experience with the city and with African American folks," Paul told me, "which I'd had little experience with prior to that."

Throughout its brief trip, First Congregational's all-white youth group partnered with an African American youth group from Milwaukee. Although the students differed in skin color, they soon learned just how much they had in common. They played basketball, discussed the riots, and even enjoyed a dance. "Afterwards Jim talked about the experience with us," Paul recalled. "Not so much what it meant, but how we felt about it. This was very much in line with Jim's pastoral style. He didn't tell people *what* to think, he simply helped them think things through."

"And eventually he told you about his time on the Freedom Rides?" I asked.

"Eventually," Paul replied.

Jim and Paul were discussing Paul's college options when midway through the conversation Jim offhandedly mentioned the transformative experience he had undergone while at Fisk. As they continued to chat, Jim revealed more and more about his participation in the civil rights movement, culminating with his role in the Freedom Rides. It was a rare admission. Most of the congregants from that era claimed they knew nothing of Jim's time on the bus.

"So where were you when he told you all this?" I asked Paul.

"Well," Paul answered, eyeing the room, "I think it was actually right here."

"Right here?" My eyes widened. "In *this* room?"

"Right here," Paul repeated.

=====

A few months earlier, on a warm Sunday in July, I had visited the First Congregational Church for the first time. I hadn't attended a church in years, but I deemed this research: a chance to hear a sermon in Jim Zwerg's former spiritual home. I took a seat near the back, and although I tried to blend in (even selecting the less popular eight o'clock morning service), I immediately stuck out among the early risers. As Reverend Mark Pirazzini began his sermon, I couldn't help but envision Jim standing behind a similar podium decades earlier, offering his own spiritual guidance.

On this day, the sermon was from the Gospel of John—specifically, the story of Jesus feeding an entire crowd with five loaves of bread and two fish. Later, Jesus walked on water to greet his disciples in their rocking boat, and his presence alone was enough to steady the waters. The reverend read from the scriptures, describing how Jesus boarded the boat and how he and his disciples eventually "reached the land towards which they were going."

Once more I thought of Jim, but this time my mind's eye pictured him not as a pastor behind a podium but as a twenty-one-year-old college kid from Wisconsin. For a time, that's all he was—just a college kid like all the rest. But then one day he boarded a bus during a tumultuous time and stayed steady as long as he could. As a result of his injuries, Jim never quite reached the land toward which he was going, although the greater movement did. Despite this victory, to this day Jim regrets his inability to continue the ride alongside his brothers and sisters.

In 2001 he received a second chance. In celebration of the fortieth anniversary of the Freedom Rides, Jim and several of his compatriots boarded a bus together one last time, leaving from Atlanta to retrace portions of the original route. Along the way they paid a visit to the Birmingham Civil Rights Institute, where Jim gazed at black-and-white photographs of the people he once counted among his friends. As he passed a time line on a wall, he was startled to see his own photograph staring back, a younger version of himself lying unconscious in a Montgomery hospital bed.

"I lost it," Jim told me. "I just lost it. I started crying and said, 'I don't deserve this. I didn't do that much.' So many people had continued on, . . . had literarily dedicated their lives. I felt I shouldn't have this kind of [recognition]."

As he wept, fellow Freedom Rider Jim Davis engulfed him in a bear hug. "What's the matter, Brother Jim?" Davis asked. Jim told him of his regret for having to cut the ride short on account of his injuries while the others rolled on without him.

"Jim," Davis said, astonished, "you don't realize it, but your voice from that hospital bed was our call to action. You," he stressed, holding his brother tightly, "you were with us the whole way."

Figure 3. Susan Wilbur, 1960.

Used by permission of Susan Wamsley.

2

Susan Wilbur

Nashville, Tennessee

"I couldn't really fathom a situation where there were people who hated me so much they wouldn't have cared at all if I had been killed."

One afternoon in the spring of 1960, seventeen-year-old Susan Wilbur glanced up from her homework to find her mother, a commercial artist, having returned home from work visibly shaken. "What is it?" Susan asked.

"They're having demonstrations downtown," her mother replied, "and I'm afraid somebody's going to get hurt."

Somebody *would* get hurt. In fact, plenty of people got hurt. Nashville's 1960 lunch-counter sit-ins were quick to rile up segregationists, whose rage intensified the following year when demonstrators set their sights on integrating movie theaters as well. Yet Susan, a senior in high school at the time, found herself far more interested in her boyfriend and the prom than the fight for civil rights. Years later she realized that her minor concerns were a privilege rarely extended to her African American counterparts. For them, the weight of the world was much greater. It wasn't until Susan began participating in demonstrations herself in the coming months that she was able to face a difficult truth: when you aren't the target of racism, it's easy to overlook it—it's like it's not even there.

═══

I called Susan on a Sunday in October, anxious to hear her story. As a white female Freedom Rider, she would offer a unique perspective, one I had rarely heard before. Now seventy-two, she picked up the phone on the second ring and began with a bit of background. "I grew up in Nashville," she said, "so I was always a southerner."

She was quick to note, however, that her childhood was anything but typical of the white southern experience. Her father died when she was four years old, leaving her to be raised in a single-parent household. Adding to her atypical experience was the fact that her mother was a southern transplant from Maryland whose attitudes about race were more progressive than those of many of her neighbors. "We never heard any derogatory remarks at all," said Susan, whose surname is now Wamsley. Rather, she and her older sister, Liz, remained mostly unaware of the racial problems that plagued their city. However, once the sit-ins began in 1960, the truth became unavoidable.

During the next several months Susan's social consciousness grew. Her eyes had suddenly opened, exposing the dark underbelly of the city she'd always loved. By the fall of 1960, Nashville seemed like a different place. Susan left her mother's home to follow in her sister's footsteps by enrolling in Nashville's Peabody College—a tree-lined teachers' school within a stone's throw of Vanderbilt University. Susan's sister, Liz, a junior at Peabody, had recently grown interested in civil rights as well, and when the two young women received word of an informational meeting hosted by the Nashville Student Movement, they decided to attend.

As Susan and Liz learned upon their arrival, the meeting was far more than informational; in fact, the movement leaders were actively recruiting volunteers for the forthcoming fight to integrate Nashville's movie theaters. As the student leaders spoke, Susan and Liz leaned forward in their chairs, absorbing every word. "We'd always sort of been told that African Americans weren't treated fairly, but this was the first time that anyone ever talked to us about doing anything about it," Susan told me. "And so we joined the movement."

To an outsider such as myself, Susan's transformation seems remarkable. How, I wondered, does a young woman mostly unaware of civil rights suddenly become actively engaged in just a few months?

According to Susan, no one moment spurred her newfound commitment to civil rights; rather, it was a series of moments. And after she'd had enough glimpses of the many inequities in her community—revealed through lunch counters, drinking fountains, and bus seats—the problems were no longer so easy to overlook. Eventually these glimpses led her down a path shared by many other Nashville-based demonstrators she came to befriend, including Jim Zwerg, John Lewis, and Diane Nash.

The following spring, once the mission to integrate the city's movie theaters was complete, she tested her commitment yet again by taking her place in a bus station ticket line and steeling herself for the dangers that lay ahead.

=====

Susan's changing perceptions of Nashville were hardly hers alone. It was nearly impossible for locals *not* to sense that Nashville was a city in flux. "It was an interesting place," Susan told me. "It was definitely southern, but it was not the Deep South. It was not like Alabama or Mississippi."

Certainly this was true in terms of violence. Although Nashville was the site of occasional violence, particularly in the midst of demonstrations, the damage was hardly as staggering as in cities like Birmingham, which by then had earned the nickname "Bombingham" because of the many explosions that white supremacists had set off in black churches and homes. Institutional racism was still prevalent in Nashville, but that was harder to trace. So too was the reason Nashville was different from other southern cities, but one factor may have been city pride. "If Atlanta was 'the city too busy to hate,'" historian Benjamin Houston remarked, citing the city's motto, "Nashville may well have termed itself 'the city too well-bred to hate.'"

To put it differently: Many of Nashville's white citizens viewed themselves as too good to resort to violence. Yet to these citizens, as they readily admitted, the city's newly emboldened African American population was indeed a problem, and with each passing day it was a growing one. After all, they believed, there were power structures to preserve, not to mention traditions.

What made Nashville unique—and perhaps what most ensured that it would be a hotbed of civil rights activity—was its role as a hub of higher education. By 1960 Nashville was home to more than a dozen colleges and universities, including four historically black institutions: Fisk University, Tennessee Agricultural and Industrial State College, the American Baptist Theological Seminary, and Meharry Medical College. As a result Nashville had more than earned its nickname "The Athens of the South." The city was proud of its educated populace and, moreover, considered itself an example of what a southern city could be—especially if willing to adopt a progressive economic and social agenda. The city surely had its problems, but Nashville's leaders appeared to be aware of them. And they knew how quickly their progress would evaporate if their city, like so many others, turned a blind eye to racial violence.

After their initial recruitment meeting, the Wilbur sisters regularly returned to Reverend Kelly Miller Smith's First Baptist Church, the epicenter of the Nashville Student Movement. The modest brick structure was on the north side of town, which meant that the sisters had to venture into a black neighborhood. Nevertheless, Susan and Liz soon grew comfortable there and regularly crossed the invisible demarcation line that unofficially segregated their city. "Everyone was very nice to us, very accepting," Susan reflected. "We really liked the kids. We literally had never known any black kids before."

This didn't mean that the Wilbur family had no experience with African Americans. Rather, the young women had simply never shared such a close relationship founded on an equal footing. "Growing up," Susan noted, "we had a woman who'd come to our house. It's always embarrassing to talk about having a black woman come to your house to clean, because it sounds so stereotypical, but she did. Her name was Viola, and she did the ironing and that sort of thing."

As a child, Susan remained naive to Viola's hardships. To her Viola was simply the woman who helped her mother keep house. But she was more than that: she occasionally doubled as a nanny as well, even taking the Wilbur sisters back to her home on the nights their mother worked late. "She lived in what everybody called the projects in those days, which I'm sure was public housing," Susan said. "I remember my sister and I going one time when I was pretty young. My mother said Liz came home saying, 'We got to sit in the back of the bus!'" Susan laughed. "And I'm sure we did. We sat with Viola in the back of the bus."

Years later, as her daughters' activism began to grow, Susan's mother maintained her unwavering support for their cause, despite the risks. "People talk to me occasionally about how brave I was," Susan told me, "but really, the brave person in all of this was my mom"—not only because of the physical violence she knew her daughters might face, but also because of her own safety.

"We had some threats, phone calls, that sort of thing," Susan remembered, "but our neighbors really stood by us and by her." Although the Wilburs' progressive views were at odds with the rest of the neighborhood, many of the family's neighbors placed friendship above their views on civil rights; one neighbor even went so far as to keep his gun ready in the event that the threats turned real.

Yet the threat that Susan's mother took most seriously had nothing to do with physical violence but concerned economic security. She feared she might lose her job—the family's sole source of income—if others learned about her daughters' activism. To make matters worse, by openly supporting her daughters she risked her relationship with her church, a congregation that openly criticized the "outside agitators." In short, Susan's mother had much to lose and little to gain, but above all she placed her faith in her daughters.

I can't help but contrast the different levels of support offered by the Zwerg and Wilbur parents. Both families found themselves in a rather distinctive situation: being the parents of white demonstrators fighting for civil rights. Yet despite this commonality they responded quite differently. In our phone conversation, Jim Zwerg had spoken candidly about his parents' lack of support—how rather than cheer him on from the sidelines, his mother accused him of worsening his father's heart condition by his actions. According to Susan, her mother took the opposite approach: remaining steadfastly in her daughters' corner and burying the fear she felt.

Fifty-five years removed from the situation, I am hardly in a position to condemn or celebrate either response, yet their juxtaposition compels me to consider the situation personally. If my children remained committed to a cause—even one I believed in—would I support their dangerous mission? Would I be willing to cheer them on as they risked their lives to build a better world?

These questions, like most hypothetical questions, have a somewhat obvious answer—as long as they remain hypothetical. But for the Zwergs and the Wilburs, the different parental responses had real consequences. Through the benefit of hindsight, we know that both Jim and Susan survived; thus the supportive approach of Susan's mother now seems the better option. But what if they hadn't survived? Which parent(s) would have made the right choice then?

Half a century later, Susan still had a hard time understanding her mother's loyal support. She credited her mother's progressive disposition to her general sense of fair play, to a moral compass that always seemed to point toward justice. "She had it inside that the whole system of segregation—the whole system of white power—was just wrong," Susan described. "And I think my sister and I sort of learned by her example. We learned that if you can help people, you do."

She was grateful for the example that her mother set and for the fact that her mother fostered an inclusive message, even while that message was at odds with many of the white households on her block. "I always felt I was fortunate," Susan reflected, "that I didn't have to say, 'I love my mother but everything she taught me about race is wrong.'"

―――

Susan Wilbur's familial support wasn't shared by all. Salynn McCollum, another white female student from Peabody, had much in common with Susan demographically, yet upon Salynn's return from the Freedom Rides, the McCollum family made its discontent known by cutting off financial support and imperiling Salynn's education in the process. Thanks to a scholarship funded by Dr. King himself—as well as some assistance from Jim Zwerg—Salynn was able to continue her studies, though without her family's blessing.

Salynn passed away in 2014, but when she was interviewed at the Nashville Public Library in 2004, she offered insight into her troubled familial relationships. When asked if her parents were upset by her activism, Salynn laughed and said, "Yeah, that's an [understatement]."

Salynn felt this familial strain most viscerally in the days after her stint in the Birmingham City Jail in mid-May 1961. As the only white woman in the Freedom Riders' group at the time (Susan joined soon after), she was placed in a separate holding cell. There, along with twenty to thirty other white women held on an array of other charges, Salynn soon endured the usual harassment afforded Freedom Riders: taunting, name-calling and the like. Most humiliating of all, however, was the treatment she received from her father, a "good ol' boy" who in a phone call with Bull Connor had persuaded the commissioner of public safety to keep an eye on his daughter until he could retrieve her himself. "So I was not questioned, processed, charged, or anything," Salynn explained. "I was just simply held for about four days."

The other jailed Freedom Riders did not receive this "special" treatment. In fact, rather than keeping an eye on them, Bull Connor personally escorted the remaining Riders to the Alabama-Tennessee border in the dead of night and left them to fend for themselves in the middle of nowhere (more on that story later).

Yet the treatment that Salynn received was a humiliation of another sort, because it undercut her convictions related to equality. Upon her father's arrival in Birmingham, she was forced to observe the blossoming friendship between Bull Connor and the man who had raised her. They got along so splendidly, in fact, that Connor volunteered to drive the pair back to the airport. Salynn watched, dumbfounded and disillusioned by how easy it was for her father to slip into his southern skin and effortlessly befriend the man she viewed as the enemy. At the same time, she fully understood her father's chameleonlike qualities. "I mean, he was a southerner," Salynn concluded. "And I was an embarrassment."

———

As Salynn McCollum flew north with her father, the remaining Freedom Riders attempted to continue their ride. But it was hard, given the way the group was fragmenting. In the days to follow, Jim Zwerg and Paul Brooks were briefly jailed, and the remainder of the Nashville Riders were dropped near the state line. Fearing that this splintering might delay the Freedom Rides, Diane Nash began working the phones to ensure that the next wave of Riders was ready.

Susan Wilbur was a member of that wave. She left Nashville along with Susan Hermann, Bernard LaFayette Jr., and several others, many of whom arrived at Reverend Fred Shuttlesworth's Bethel Baptist Church in Birmingham just in time to welcome the Freedom Riders returning from their midnight ride with Bull Connor. If Birmingham's commissioner of public safety thought he could intimidate the Freedom Riders into turning back, he was sorely mistaken. Rather, the injustices wrought upon them recommitted them to their cause, further confirming the need to continue their journey.

Although Susan never found herself dumped on the side of an Alabama road in the dead of night, she faced her own share of intimidation. On the evening of Friday, May 19, 1961, she and her fellow Freedom Riders sat in Birmingham's Greyhound station anxiously awaiting a driver to take them to Montgomery. When no driver materialized, they were forced to continue their anguishing wait, slouching in their seats in the bus terminal as the Ku Klux Klan kept a close watch throughout the evening. The Klan intimidated the Freedom Riders as best they could—stomping their feet and spilling the Riders' drinks, for instance—but the Nashville Riders hardly flinched. They'd trained for this kind of encounter, and even though they were shaken they offered no visual clues. Instead they relied on their nonviolence training to empower them, peering into books and newspapers and conversing quietly among themselves.

Despite their efforts, it was impossible to ignore the calm-before-the-storm atmosphere that soon enveloped the terminal. The Riders were initially relieved to learn that the Klansmen had departed, but their absence only cleared the way for the police to begin their own intimidation tactics. Phone lines were disconnected, the restaurant in the terminal was closed, and the Riders soon realized that they were now being held captive by a different adversary: officers of the law.

From her place inside the station, Susan witnessed this changing of the guard with growing concern. As nightfall descended, there was no telling what violence might take place. After hearing of the previous week's Mother's Day horrors in Anniston and Birmingham, Susan knew all too well the risks she assumed just by being there. At any moment a bomb might be thrown, a blackjack swung, or a police dog let loose in the terminal. And the cover of darkness, Susan feared, would only embolden the perpetrators.

=====

As Susan and the other Freedom Riders inside the bus station were dealing with their problem, the Kennedy administration was simultaneously fighting a political proxy war on the Riders' behalf. Alabama governor John Patterson did his best to avoid the Freedom Riders' situation altogether, but when Attorney General Robert Kennedy played his trump card by threatening federal intervention, the governor at last made himself available for a call.

The conversation was hardly cordial. In fact, for much of it Kennedy found himself on the receiving end of one tirade after the next. Yet by the call's end Patterson had requested a face-to-face meeting with a Justice Department representative, and the attorney general knew just whom to send.

John Seigenthaler, who had been keeping tabs on the Freedom Riders since the Mother's Day violence a week earlier, took a seat in the governor's office on Friday, May 19. Seigenthaler had been sent to serve as President Kennedy's personal representative, and he attempted to use the weight of that office to persuade the governor to protect the Riders during their time in his state. Several of the governor's entourage, including Floyd Mann, Alabama's forty-year-old director of public safety, were present as well. As Susan and the other Riders peered at the shadowy figures looming beyond the windows of Birmingham's Greyhound terminal, Seigenthaler, two hours to the south in the state capitol, attempted to talk sense into the governor. Patterson had little patience for it. Instead he used his audience with the Justice Department representative to issue one excuse after another for why he was incapable of honoring the attorney general's request to protect the Freedom Riders during their time in his state.

After Governor Patterson made his position clear, all eyes turned to

Mann, an Alabama native, a decorated World War II veteran, and a person whose honorable service had more than earned him a place at the table. *Is it true?* Seigenthaler asked. *Is the state of Alabama incapable of protecting the Riders?* Mann respectfully disagreed with the governor's assessment, informing Seigenthaler that with the proper resources, his law enforcement officers could indeed keep the Riders safe.

If there were film footage of this moment, I imagine we would see the governor's jaw drop. Surely it must have. After all, here was one of the highest-ranking law enforcement officers in the state directly contradicting his boss. It was a breakthrough in the negotiations, and it left Governor Patterson with no cards left to play. Begrudgingly the governor began ironing out details with the federal government.

By morning, the Riders would be ready to roll.

═══

After a mostly sleepless night in the bus terminal, Susan opened her eyes and began her slow, sleepy-eyed march toward the buses with all the rest of the Riders. A driver had at last agreed to take them to Montgomery, an assignment he accepted only after learning of the governor's assurance of protection. This was great news for the Riders as well; they were safe, at least for the moment.

Susan collapsed into her bus seat, allowing herself a long overdue sigh of relief as she noticed the increased presence of patrol officers. In addition to Alabama law enforcement's robust ground force, she could hear patrol planes and helicopters flying a circuit overhead. Such an escort might have seemed excessive were it not for the violence that had occurred on Mother's Day, the previous Sunday. "We sort of believed that we were going to be fine," Susan remembered. "Then, of course, the helicopter disappeared, as did the police. By the time we got to the bus station, there was no one in sight except bad people."

As noted in chapter 1, John Lewis awakened from his slumber just as the state troopers went away, and in that moment of silence he turned to Jim Zwerg and said, "That's not good." From her place a few seats back, Susan peered out the window and saw a ghost town. The "bad people" had yet to reveal themselves, but the sense of foreboding had already taken hold.

The Riders emerged from the bus and gathered tightly around one another, and within seconds the nightmarish pandemonium began. Suddenly the ghost town of the bus terminal sprang to life: men emerged from corners, hallways, and doors, surging forward as they clutched their chains, sticks, and bats. Their goal was to land a blow, leave a mark, and remind the Riders that there was a price to pay for their behavior. But perhaps a secondary goal was to satisfy their own rage, to find a flesh-and-blood target for their hatred.

The carnage began with the journalists—*Life* magazine's Norman Ritter endured the first blows, and within seconds the violence spread to include representatives from NBC and *Time* magazine. Cameras were hurled to the ground and smashed, the film torn and exposed to the light.

Once the journalists were dealt with, the mob turned its attention to the Riders, beginning with Jim Zwerg and John Lewis as well as William Barbee, who had met the Riders at the station just a few moments earlier. Susan Wilbur and Susan Hermann watched the mob close in on the men as they themselves searched for cover. But cover was a difficult thing to find in the midst of a mob, even for a pair of white women who might more easily blend in.

Before Susan began to run she froze, held captive by the horror she witnessed just an arm's length away. There stood Jim Zwerg, his eyes closed in silent prayer. "I was standing right next to him when they hit him," she told me, her voice quavering. "They started beating him, and I—I thought he was dead. I literally thought he was dead. Because he just went down. I remember hearing him say, 'Oh God.' And then they just really lit into him."

As fists tore into Jim, John, and William, the two Susans, standing just feet away, took advantage of the momentarily distracted mob to make themselves invisible. With their heads down, they quickened their pace and attempted to infiltrate the crowd. It was an odd feeling, Susan remembered, being in the midst of so many people and knowing that nobody was there to help.

The Susans searched frantically for an escape route, and their eyes eventually landed on a taxi not far from the station. They rushed toward it alongside some African American women, including Catherine Burks and Lucretia Collins, but the women barely squeezed into the cab before the black cabbie took one look at them and refused to drive them. In Alabama it was illegal for a black cabbie to drive white passengers, even in a moment of crisis. The irony was hardly lost on the Susans, who, for perhaps the first time in their lives, were denied service as a result of their skin color.

According to Catherine, she, Lucretia, and the other black female Freedom Riders extricated themselves from the cab, refusing to leave without the Susans. At that point twenty-year-old Bernard LaFayette Jr. intervened, demanding that the black women get back in the cab and promising to help the white women find another escape. Bernard attempted to make good on his promise, but as the mob intensified, he was forced to abandon his efforts and retreat to a nearby post office, leaving the Susans alone once more.

The white women attempted to maintain their low profile: walking, never running, in the opposite direction from the bus terminal. They remained stone-faced throughout—a difficult feat, given that each step was accompanied by the screams of their fellow Riders. A few minutes later, just as they were beginning to believe they had left the chaos behind, Susan glanced back to notice a teenage boy skulking after them. He quickened his step, pulled back his fist, and sent it slamming into Susan Wilbur's skull. She bobbed forward, attracting the attention of others on the street, including a woman clutching a pocketbook. With bloodlust rising within her, the woman soon joined the beating, rushing toward the Susans and peppering them with a series of quick blows with her pocketbook. "If you think that's not much, then you don't know women's pocketbooks," Susan told me quite seriously.

Susan struggled to keep her footing, wobbling from side to side as the poundings rained upon her. As she began wondering how much more she could endure, John Seigenthaler entered the scene. At last—someone in the crowd willing to help. Seigenthaler leaped from his car, ran toward the women, and urged them into his vehicle. But Susan, unfamiliar with the stranger beckoning toward her, refused. Baffled, Seigenthaler tried again, pleading with the young women to get in the car before it was too late. "I thought," Susan explained, "if the mob sees us getting away, trying to get away, they're going to get all of us. I figured they were going to grab him, that they'd grab all of us."

Seigenthaler warned the women that they would surely be hurt if they didn't get in the car immediately, but still Susan Wilbur refused, causing Susan Hermann to hesitate as well. "Maybe I was being noble," Susan reflected fifty-five years later, "but—your mind—it's weird. You're sort of operating on instinct. You don't know what you're going to do."

In retrospect, Susan attributed her refusal to take Seigenthaler up on his offer as the result of sheer terror. "I'd never even seen a fistfight in my life, you know? And suddenly you're around all this violence, right in the middle of it." Not only was she in the middle of it, she herself was a target. "I couldn't really fathom a situation where there were people who hated me so much they wouldn't have cared at all if I had been killed," Susan remarked.

Seigenthaler continued to plead with Susan right up until the moment he spotted a pipe-wielding man rushing toward him. "Get back!" Seigenthaler hollered at him. "I'm with the federal government!" If his admission had any effect, it probably only compelled the man to swing a little harder. An instant later the pipe struck Seigenthaler directly behind his left ear, turning his world to darkness.

The assault was as barbaric as it was revealing: a confirmation to the Kennedy administration that the mobs in Alabama had grown so emboldened that they hardly thought twice before assaulting a federal official in broad daylight just blocks from the state capitol. About ten minutes later, as Seigenthaler faded in and out of consciousness, the Montgomery police came across his body lying beside the car.

"So they start going through his stuff," Susan recounted, "and one officer finds some kind of government documentation and says, 'Who's that Kennedy fella?,' and I guess John was awake enough to say, 'He's the president of the United States.'"

Realizing that the mob had beaten the wrong man—a man with direct ties to the White House, no less—one of the officers shouted, "Get this man to the hospital!"

Susan laughed as she reached this point in the story, but then her laughter quickly subsided. "I'm not making light of it," she told me. "It was a very terrifying, scary thing. But there were light moments here and there"—though admittedly not enough of them.

After Seigenthaler's bludgeoning, the Susans continued their escape, their shoes clicking down the sidewalk as they attempted to distance themselves from the fray. As they began to approach local businesses, they watched as one proprietor after another refused them entrance. *So much for blending in*, Susan thought.

At last they reached a store that allowed them not only to enter but also to use their phone. Susan stared at the numbers and wondered whom she might call for help. Eventually she settled on the police, who seemed like the logical choice—although given the Freedom Riders' past experiences with law enforcement, perhaps it might have been more pragmatic to call Diane Nash, who was already at work coordinating the next wave of Riders.

Susan placed a follow-up call to Nash a few minutes later, and the young organizer immediately began making arrangements for the Susans to return to Nashville by train. But there was still the matter of how to get to the train station.

When the police arrived, the Susans learned that the officers were happy to assist—anything to get the Freedom Riders out of town. The young women were placed in the back of the squad car and driven to the train station. After a moment of silence, one of the officers turned to face Susan Wilbur. "So," he asked, "is one of those niggers your boyfriend?"

"No, my boyfriend's in the service," Susan replied, which was the truth.

"Well, I'll tell you one thing," the officer said, turning back around. "If you were my daughter, I'd put a bullet between your eyes."

═══

Today, Susan explained, it's difficult for young people to understand what life was like back then. She told me how her ten-year-old granddaughter, Olivia, recently interviewed her for a school project and how excited Olivia had been to tell her friends about her grandmother the Freedom Rider—even if only a few of those friends knew what a Freedom Rider was.

"That must've been a proud moment for you," I said.

"Oh absolutely, absolutely," Susan agreed. "It's probably one of the proudest moments I've had. When she was in front of her class telling about it, that made it all worth it."

I nodded. "When you think back on those days," I asked, "what stands out? Is there a single moment that resonates?"

Susan paused, considered, and rewound the tape in her head. There were so many moments, she explained, that it was difficult for her to pick just one. "The one thing I remember," she said at last, "is Bernard LaFayette and James Bevel. I just remember being in a church and everyone singing, 'We Shall Overcome.' And, of course, those guys just had incredible voices, and they sounded so good together."

Susan paused before continuing. "It made us feel like we were really brothers and sisters, you know? And it was a wonderful feeling because it opened up a whole new experience for us. In the end, it had a purpose. It was social, but you also really felt that you were doing something that mattered."

Night after night Susan and the other demonstrators sang. And together they hit all the right notes.

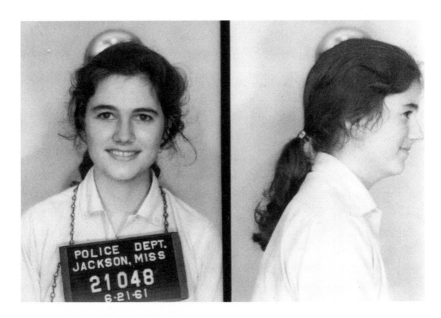

Figure 4. Miriam Feingold, mug shot, June 21, 1961.

Mississippi State Sovereignty Commission, "Mississippi State Sovereignty Commission Photograph," June 21, 1961, SCRID# 2-55-5-48-1-1-1ph, Series 2515: Mississippi State Sovereignty Commission Records, 1994–2006, Mississippi Department of Archives and History, February 20, 2017, https://www.mdah.ms.gov/arrec/digital_archives/sovcom/photo.php?display=item&oid=226.

3

Miriam Feingold

Brooklyn, New York

*"They were waving their fists in the air, and it was clear
they were screaming at us. We couldn't hear what, exactly,
because the bus windows were closed, but I can assure you it
was not 'Welcome to Montgomery.'"*

In some ways Miriam (Mimi) Feingold seemed destined to be a Freedom
Rider. She was born into a left-leaning Jewish household in Brooklyn, the
daughter of nonconformist parents, both of whom strongly supported
civil rights issues. Her father, a math teacher at a local high school, and her
mother, a librarian, were both active in the Teachers' Union, which easily
made them targets in the midst of the McCarthy era. Despite what Mimi
later described as the "stifling conformity" of 1950s America, her parents
refused to conform. They were proud of their outsider status, even if it put
them at risk.

As a young girl Mimi often fell asleep to the sound of Teachers' Union
members strategizing in the living room of her family's apartment. "There's
something very soothing about going to bed to the murmuring of adult
voices," Mimi told me during a phone interview. "I have no idea what they
were discussing, but they were political meetings of some kind."

After many nights of falling asleep to such chatter, her parents' activism eventually began to rub off on her. Mimi's entrance to the world of
activism had little to do with education-related issues, however; instead
they stemmed from her moral disapproval of nuclear tests. Throughout her
teenage years Mimi occasionally attended protest rallies and marches, but
much to her disappointment she soon learned that even in the heart of New
York City there were surprisingly few avenues of protest available to her. "In

other words," Mimi said, "I was wound up and ready to go, but there was no place to go."

I was shocked by this realization: somehow, in the most populated city in the country, there were few outlets to make oneself heard. How could that be? I wondered. Wasn't New York City the epicenter of activism? Not in the 1950s Cold War era, Mimi explained, especially with McCarthyism run amok.

An exception occurred in 1954, when in celebration of the *Brown v. Board of Education* ruling Mimi helped organize a busload of her fellow students to attend the Youth March for Integrated Schools in Washington, DC. It was Mimi's first bus-related demonstration experience, though far from her last.

====

In the fall of 1959 Mimi's commitment to social justice followed her to Swarthmore College in southeastern Pennsylvania. She was quick to join the campus's Political Action Committee, but much as with her experiences in New York, she soon found the protest scene to be less than thriving. "We cast about for things to do," Miriam noted, "and in the very beginning we didn't do much more but support the Quakers and peace movement in Philadelphia. But soon after, things broke loose, and that was due to the student sit-ins."

For progressive students like Mimi, the sit-ins in Greensboro, North Carolina, and beyond were proof that young people were capable of making real change. "Here were people actually *doing* something," Mimi declared—a stark contrast to the endless meetings and conversations that had passed for activism in Swarthmore's Political Action Committee. The direct action she observed throughout the sit-ins fascinated her and compelled her to give herself more fully to the cause.

Since Swarthmore wasn't home to a Woolworth's, Mimi and her fellow demonstrators targeted the closest one they could find, which was just four miles south in the city of Chester. Their efforts were part of a nationwide effort by the National Association for the Advancement of Colored People (NAACP) to boycott all Woolworth's and Kresge's locations, even those that had integrated their lunch counters. "We used to go down every weekend," Mimi reported, "and we would picket Woolworth's in support of the boycott. It was fulfilling that we were finally doing something, but it was still distant. We still weren't in the middle of it."

Anxious to find her way to where the action was, Mimi began commuting to CORE headquarters during her 1961 spring break; the office was at 38 Park Row in Manhattan, just a subway ride away from her home in

Brooklyn. The office's proximity and purpose provided a unique spring break opportunity for the young college student.

Although Mimi was new to CORE, CORE was hardly new to the country. In fact, it had been founded nearly two decades earlier, in the spring of 1942. CORE's long history of activism seemed to ensure its future role on the civil rights battlefield. Yet unbeknownst to Mimi, as she sat at her desk at CORE headquarters, she had actually taken a front-row seat in an organization in flux. James Farmer, who had recently accepted CORE's national directorship, anxiously began to chart his organization's future, and it was an uncertain one. Where would CORE focus its battles? And how would it fight them?

As Mimi continued her clerical work at the CORE office, she began hearing whispers of a proposed bus ride through the South that was intended to test the enforcement of a pair of Supreme Court decisions, both of which had ruled in favor of integrated bus travel. To many, this proposed ride seemed a novel idea, even though CORE had organized a similar ride in the spring of 1947. As noted in the prologue, CORE had teamed up with various other civil rights organizations to oversee the Journey of Reconciliation, an integrated bus trip through the upper South, beginning in Washington, DC, and including stops in Virginia, North Carolina, Tennessee, and Kentucky. The Journey of Reconciliation Riders, though successful in reaching their destinations, received far less media attention than they had hoped for. Thus, their success was only partial. What good was their journey, after all, if their efforts were mostly unknown?

The Freedom Rides built upon CORE's earlier effort; only this time the Riders were assigned to test two Supreme Court decisions including the 1960 *Boynton v. Virginia* ruling (which confirmed that white-only facilities—even the restaurants and bathrooms within the bus terminals—were in violation of the Interstate Commerce Clause).

Another difference between the Rides was that this time the proposed itinerary included Georgia, Alabama, and Mississippi—a Deep South route that was all but certain to draw attention. It certainly drew Mimi's. "Needless to say, my antenna went zipping way up," Mimi told me. "Here was something where I could actually be doing something definite—meeting the energy head-on, not rolling bandages far from the front. So I signed up. I filled out the application, and they accepted me. The rest, as they say, is history."

In June 1961 Judy Frieze (a recent Smith College graduate) and Mimi boarded a bus from New York to Atlanta to meet several other newly recruited Freedom Riders. Along with the new recruits were a few civil rights veterans as well, most notably thirty-one-year-old Wyatt Tee Walker—the light-skinned, bespectacled executive director of the Southern Christian Leadership Conference (SCLC). Later praised by Dr. King for his intellectual prowess, Walker is perhaps best remembered for his administrative and organizational skills—attributes that were often overlooked but that were ultimately crucial to the movement's success.

Yet on the June morning when they began their journey, Walker was just another Freedom Rider. He and his wife, Theresa, took their seats among Mimi and the others; all of them were anxious to begin their journey to Jackson, Mississippi. Although New Orleans had been the original destination of the CORE-sponsored Freedom Rides, in the aftermath of the beatings and the bus firebombing the destination was changed.

As a result of secret negotiations between Attorney General Robert Kennedy and Mississippi governor Ross Barnett, the governor had agreed to ensure the Riders' safety during their time in his state. But there was a catch: they would be safe, Barnett promised, but they would also be promptly arrested upon entering the capital. There was no such deal struck with the government of Alabama, through which the Riders had to pass to reach Mississippi.

True to his word, Governor Barnett ensured that busloads of Riders soon filled the Jackson City Jail, the Hinds County Jail, and finally, by mid-June, the notorious Mississippi prison known as Parchman Farm. Given Barnett's reputation as a segregationist, perhaps this deal was the best one that Attorney General Kennedy could have struck. Still, many of the Riders felt betrayed by what they viewed as a backroom deal that ensured their safety only while they were behind bars. They had expected this sort of treatment from Barnett—a prowhite, card-carrying member of the Citizens' Council—but Kennedy was supposed to be their ally. To many Riders the deal felt suspiciously expedient, dealing with the Freedom Rider "problem" without actually addressing the larger issues the Riders had hoped to publicize.

Mimi was both a beneficiary and a victim of the deal: she was safe, but she was also headed to prison. Before arriving there, however, she first had to endure Alabama. "The bus trip from Atlanta to Montgomery was, all things considered, relatively uneventful," Mimi recalled. "I don't remember much. It was our arrival in Montgomery that I remember very, very vividly."

The afternoon of June 20 was sweltering, even by Alabama standards. As the bus slowed to a halt at Montgomery's Trailways bus station, Mimi peered out the window and spotted throngs of white people crowded behind makeshift sawhorse barricades, their faces red and twisted in rage. Not a single act of violence had been committed, but already the scene had turned ugly—just as it had for the many Freedom Riders who had come before and just as it would for the many who would come after.

"The state troopers all looked like something out of Hollywood's central casting," Mimi described, "complete with beer bellies hanging over their belt buckles and cowboy hats on their heads. And the crowd was not exactly friendly looking. They were waving their fists in the air, and it was clear they were screaming at us. We couldn't hear what, exactly, because the bus windows were closed, but I can assure you it was not 'Welcome to Montgomery.'"

Mimi's eyes shifted from the troopers to the crowd and then back to the troopers. As she and the other Riders peered nervously out the window, the driver—apparently unwilling to place his faith in the sawhorse barricades—steered the bus clear of the station and parked instead in a nearby dry cleaner's lot. He flung the door wide, then urged the Riders to leave. They did, and they were immediately corralled into a parade of waiting vehicles. Mimi and Judy were ushered into a car driven by their host family, a black couple whose names are lost to history.

"Lie low," the man ordered, and Mimi and Judy shrunk down in the seats. It was indeed a necessary precaution. As Susan Wilbur had learned during her own stint in Montgomery a few weeks earlier, not only was it illegal for a black man to chauffer a white woman, but in the eyes of many southerners it was an unforgivable cultural violation as well. Nevertheless, the black couple drove the white women in spite of the risk—their own act of heroism.

Hunkered down, Mimi and Judy felt the car weave through the Montgomery streets and were tugged backward and forward each time the car had to stop and start at a traffic light. Eventually the car came to a halt in front of a house in the black section of Montgomery. The women peeked up for the first time and spotted a lovely middle class home before them. "It was beautifully decorated," Mimi said. "They had this gorgeous huge picture window that looked down onto the street."

Enticing as the view from that spot inside the house probably was, their hosts urged Mimi and Judy to keep their distance from that window. If a car happened to drive by and spot white women in their home, they explained, there was no telling what retribution might come. "They were sticking their necks way out just to take us in," Mimi said, and since the last thing she or Judy wanted to do was to put them at risk, the young women indeed steered clear of the window.

Despite the precautionary measures, Mimi had a hard time understanding why their being there was such a violation. Perhaps it was naïveté, or youthful idealism, but it wasn't until later that evening that it occurred to her that the black couple had probably never hosted white people in their home, let alone a pair of white female northerners. "It was a challenge for them, I think, to figure out how to deal with us," Mimi said.

That night, as Mimi and Judy gathered in the formal dining room for dinner, they were surprised to find their hosts unwilling to eat with them; instead, the couple insisted on eating in the kitchen. "Oh, we'll eat with you in the kitchen then," Mimi insisted. "There's no need to dirty up a whole other room here." But the couple politely refused. Puzzled but unwilling to press the matter, Mimi and Judy soon found themselves dining alone, using their hosts' finest china; the sound of scraping silverware was a reminder of the awkwardness that had developed.

At breakfast the following morning the culture clash revealed itself even more prominently. Once again the hosts refused to eat with their guests, but not only was the custom foreign this time, so was the food itself. Although Mimi and Judy were no strangers to the sausage, eggs, coffee, and juice spread out before them, they were completely baffled by the bowl of "white stuff" placed on the table.

Mimi and Judy shot each other a look, curious how best to handle the unnamed food. Eventually the women concluded it must be some sort of hot cereal, but since they'd only been given plates, they didn't know where to put their servings of it. *Perhaps you eat it as you would mashed potatoes*, Mimi thought, and tested her theory by scooping a helping onto her plate and using her spoon to form a well. Then she reached for the cream, filled the well, sprinkled some sugar on top, and proceeded to eat her "hot cereal."

A few minutes into the meal their female host entered the dining room to check on her guests and was surprised to find the young women eating grits mashed-potato style, a far cry from the way the black couple typically ate theirs. "And to this day I am in awe of her self-control," Mimi chuckled, "that she did not at that point fall on the floor laughing at what we had done."

═══

On June 21 Mimi returned to the Trailways bus terminal in Montgomery with eight other Freedom Riders—three white and five black—all of whom remained fully committed to the cause that stretched before them. Yet their commitment hardly safeguarded them from their fear. Mimi and the other Riders anxiously awaited to board the bus, and their wait extended even longer when the original driver refused to get behind the wheel. As the Riders waited for a replacement driver, the bus station's uncomfortable silence was interrupted by a short popping sound erupting throughout the terminal. A cry went up, and as the Riders instinctually ducked, law enforcement suddenly came alive. Everyone assumed the popping sound was a gunshot, but after a cursory investigation the police determined it was a firecracker. The Riders exhaled a collective sigh of relief. They were safe again, for the moment.

When they boarded the bus soon after, the Riders were faced with a different problem. Their bus driver, though willing to drive them, refused to make any unnecessary stops. He also demanded that all the Freedom Riders sit in the back. Despite his insistence on the matter, Mimi recalls being quite surprised by the many stops they did make along the way. "It was the milk run," she told me, the local route rather than the express route. "So we stopped at every little two-bit town or crossroads."

Passengers boarded at almost every stop, and as the bus filled up, several of the local black riders glanced back to notice something clearly awry: there were white people, Mimi included, seated in the back. "Then an interesting thing began to happen," Mimi noted. The local black riders seated in the back began asking what was happening, and word of the Freedom Riders' message soon began to spread. Mimi got the sense that the local black riders' curiosity shifted to gratitude. By the act of sitting where and with whom they chose, the Freedom Riders had inspired others to consider their own future role in furthering the cause of civil rights. In witnessing the Freedom Riders' so-called defiance, they themselves were set free.

Mimi recalled one young African American rider in particular, who, upon boarding the bus, was soon changed. "He was one of the standing-room-only crowd," Mimi told me. "And by this point it was getting close to lunch or early afternoon, and he had this huge picnic basket with him." He was on leave from the military, and the basket had been thrust into his arms by his mother, who understood all too well that a restaurant in the South would be unlikely to serve him. Thus the food in that basket was meant to last him all the way back to his base. "He insisted on turning the entire contents of that basket over to us," Mimi stated. "He *insisted*. So we feasted on fried chicken and corn bread and some sort of greens. It was delicious."

Then the soldier also insisted that the Freedom Riders take the meal's crown jewel with them: a chocolate layer cake tucked tightly in a pink bakery box and secured with a string. Throughout the entirety of the ride—all the way to the Hinds County Jail in Jackson, Mississippi—Mimi served as the keeper of that cake. She held on to that box as if her life depended on it, protecting it over every bump throughout Alabama and Mississippi. "The minute we hit the Hinds County Jail, we shared that cake," Mimi declared proudly. "It seemed [like] an unbelievable privilege."

It was. And it was the last one they would receive for some time.

═══

Throughout June and July, as the buses continued to flood Jackson, local law enforcement began fine-tuning its arrest procedures. Within days it had it down to a science. The Freedom Riders exited the bus, entered the bus station's whites-only waiting room, and upon being informed that they were in breach of the peace, were placed in the backs of paddy wagons and driven to the Jackson City Jail. "It was a choreographed dance," Mimi recalled, which ensured that the inevitable narrative always played out. In some ways this inevitability was to the Riders' benefit: it was a practiced protocol that left little room for surprises.

Mimi and her fellow Riders arrived at the Jackson City Jail on Wednesday, June 21, another sweltering day in the state capital. Upon their arrival the white Riders—Mimi, Judy Frieze, and Margaret Burr Leonard—were immediately segregated from their black counterparts and were herded through the booking process, which included fingerprinting and mug shots. "At every stage, every deputy would have some derogatory thing to say to us," Mimi recalled. "Like, 'Oh, so you're a commie.' Or, to the women, and what they said to me: 'Oh, so you date niggers.'" Yet as a result of their non-violence training, Mimi and the other Riders knew better than to take the bait. She bit her lip, refused to engage the hecklers, and allowed the herding to continue.

Near the end of the booking process Mimi was led to a small office, where a booking officer began running her through a list of questions: name, age, and city of origin, among others. When they got to the question of religion, Mimi hesitated. "That was one of those moments in my life when time sort of stood still," she remembered. "The problem was that although I was raised in a Jewish family, we were not religious, by any means. We were not practicing. So I was raised sort of on the agnostic end of religion. And that was one possibility. I could say I was an atheist or agnostic. Or I could tell the truth and say I was Jewish."

Both options held risks, and for Mimi it was simply a question of which answer might least offend the southern Christian police officer. "I was just a teeny-weeny bit apprehensive," Mimi explained. "Any time I was separated from the group like that, I was never 100 percent sure where I'd end up."

A third option was to give what she assumed was the right answer and simply claim to be a Christian. Yet for Mimi it felt wrong to hide behind a lie to ensure her safety, to deny a part of herself to please her captor. "What it finally boiled down to was my gut," she told me. "I could not deny that I was Jewish."

Once she had stated that she was Jewish, the man peered up at her, a sneer crossing his face. "Oh," he hissed, "so you're a Jewess." Though the word hadn't always been considered derogatory, by the time the officer used it, it had certainly taken on negative connotations—most notably by drawing attention to, as writer Daniel Krieger put it, "prevailing stereotypes about Jewish women's bewitching and exotic sensuality."

"Of all the reactions," Mimi said, "that's the one I never expected. I'm not sure I'd ever even heard the word." Yet one thing was certain: he hadn't meant it as a compliment.

=====

As procedure dictated, the following day Mimi and the other Freedom Riders were transferred to the Hinds County Jail. Once again they were segregated by race, as well as by sex. Their meeting in the cell served as a spiritual reunion of sorts, a chance to reconvene with like-minded people wedded to a common cause. Unexpectedly, coming together even under such circumstances had a positive effect on morale. It was a reminder that they were hardly alone. Because of their numbers (Mimi estimates there were twenty people in a cell built for eight), they were woefully short on bunks; nevertheless, their goodwill remained in high supply.

"The people who got the bunk beds were the people who needed them," Mimi explained, citing "those who were older or had a special situation."

The others made do with mattresses on the concrete floor. "In a lot of ways it was like going to summer camp or something," Mimi said. "It wasn't, of course," she was quick to add, although the close quarters, camaraderie, and highly structured days did in fact lend themselves to the comparison. "By the time we'd gotten there, the girls in the cell had already started to put a structure to the day," she stated. "There were quiet periods, and there were activity periods."

The activity periods in particular did much to provide the intellectually stimulating experiences the women yearned for. Although they lacked the resources many of the university-educated women had become accustomed to, they hardly lacked "course offerings." Everyone, it seemed, had an area of expertise, and as a result the imprisoned women were treated to an array of classes: French, Greek, and even ballet. The only book available to them was the Bible, and so, regardless of religion, many of the women enjoyed Bible readings.

After a few days their classes were put on hold because they were transferred to their final stop: Parchman Farm. "The Hinds County Jail had made arrangements with the state of Mississippi to rent part of the state penitentiary because they were getting very, very overcrowded," Mimi explained. "It was bad enough on the women's side, but the men's side was even worse."

Yet easing the jail's overcrowding was but one motivation for the transfer; the state had an ulterior motive as well. "This was an opportunity to intimidate us even more by sending us off to the dreaded Parchman penitentiary," Mimi said. For prosegregation southerners, it probably seemed a fitting punishment for the northern rabble-rousers: a one-way ticket to a place no one wanted to be.

====

Situated on twenty thousand acres in Mississippi's Sunflower County, Parchman Farm (as it would soon be known) began operations in 1904, serving as the state's only prison exclusively for black men (though by 1917, the prison housed both black and white men and women). In the beginning, Parchman was set up as a revenue earner for the state, a chance for Mississippi to profit from convict labor. And profit it did. According to historian William Banks Taylor, by 1905, just a year into its operations, the prison farm had earned $185,000 (about $4.9 million in 2009 dollars, writer John Buntin estimates). It was only the beginning.

By 1919 Parchman had become the most profitable prison farm in the country. The annual congress of the American Prison Association noted that the previous year the prison had earned a net revenue of $825,000. "Given its total of 1,200 prisoners—and subtracting invalids, cripples, [and] incompetents—it made a profit over $800 for each working prisoner," the association confirmed.

It was a business model that incentivized the prosecution of black men. Why pay for labor, after all, when you could get it for free? Such a model was exploitative on every level, yet few white southerners batted an eye. After all, southern economics had long benefited from systems such as this, most obviously the institution of slavery. To some extent the prison farm served as the South's answer to emancipation. If slavery was illegal, then southerners would simply rely on black convicts to serve as modern state-sanctioned slaves.

By 1961 Parchman was already a different place. And it was soon to be changed further, once the Freedom Riders began packing the cells.

═══

As unlikely as it sounds, when Mimi arrived at Parchman in late June, she felt an odd sort of relief. "I do have to say, in a weird sort of way," Mimi admitted, "we felt safer once we were in jail than when we were out on the open roads. The whole time riding in the paddy wagon—as we drove through very remote areas where all we saw was farmland and forest—I just kept imagining, I mean, we all did, that somewhere along the line the bus would pull along a deserted side road and that would be the end of that." Yet Mimi's worst fear never materialized, and after a 150-mile drive north, she and the other Riders arrived at Parchman unscathed.

At this working prison farm, the majority of prisoners lived in cabins on the property, dedicating their days to growing and farming their food and returning to their cabins each evening. Yet even the freedom to work outside was a luxury the Freedom Riders were denied. Instead the warden decided that a more fitting punishment was to keep them locked in their cells in the maximum security unit.

By the time she arrived at Parchman Mimi had already become adept at handling the protocols of incarceration. After receiving the standard-issue black-and-white-striped cotton skirt, mattress, sheet, pillow, and cup, she was swiftly escorted to her cell.

Like the Hinds County Jail, Parchman maintained segregated cells. As such, Mimi shared hers with Judy Frieze and another white female Rider. Together the women made the most of their situation, although the lack of exercise began to wear away at their morale. At the outset, hard labor in the burning Mississippi sun hardly seemed the preferred option, but as the days dragged on Mimi grew more and more desperate for physical exercise. She and others soon found themselves walking back and forth in the cell, counting their steps, aiming for a mile each day even within that confined space.

Although the lack of exercise was a problem, it paled in comparison to the general sense of monotony that soon overtook the ward. At best the Freedom Riders had pencils, paper, and a Bible, and as a result of such limited possessions they relied on their creativity for entertainment. Though separated by cells, the women remained a tight-knit community. Much as they had done in the Hinds County Jail, they divided their day into quiet time and activity time, the latter including Bible readings, testimonials, and Mimi's favorite activity: the mock radio station on the women's ward.

Barring access to a real radio, the women's impromptu radio show seemed the next best thing. "I don't even remember if it had a name or if we just called it 'The Show,'" Mimi said. "It was a variety show. Every cell had to think up an act." Some women told jokes, others told stories, and others sang songs. "One of the things you could also think up, instead of an act, was a commercial," Mimi recalled. "Every few acts you'd break for commercial, so we'd have these commercials about the prison soap and the wonderful things it did for your complexion. 'Use Parchman borax soap bars!' The commercials, of course, were always the funniest."

Yet not even comedic commercials boosted morale better than freedom songs. The male Freedom Riders, who were housed in a separate wing of the prison, could often hear the women singing, and vice versa; their voices therefore connected them even while they remained physically apart. But the women also sang for their closer neighbors: the male inmates in maximum security. These men were rumored to be on death row, and despite their vast differences in crime and sentencing, the female Freedom Riders communicated with them.

"They just adored our singing," Mimi recalled. "And they taught us how to pass notes back and forth." The maximum-security prisoners seemed to have cracked the various codes of prison life, including how a carefully tossed note could move from one cell to another through the vent. Mimi was never clear on the logistics of this note-passing procedure, but she remembered that most of the notes' contents expressed the prisoners' gratitude for the women's songs. Despite the warden's intentional separation of the Freedom Riders from the maximum-security inmates (allegedly for the Riders' safety), the note passing and singing allowed a bond to form. The more the two groups got to know each other, the more Mimi and the other Riders began to wonder whether their separation was really about safety or the warden's attempt to ensure that the Freedom Riders' "dangerous" ideas didn't spread.

The jailers too were a unique population within the prison, and, Mimi recalled, they were often caught "between a rock and a hard place," especially when it came to interacting with the women in their ward. Many of the jailers subscribed to an "ancient notion of chivalry," Mimi called it, the belief that women "had to be protected and adored." However, their chivalric impulse became complicated when the women in question were, as Mimi put it, "outside agitator, commie, nigger-lovers."

Of course, not all jailers subscribed to such acts of paternalism. "I'm sure you've heard about the vaginal search," Mimi told me. Of the many personal violations committed upon the Freedom Riders, this one was so shocking that I hesitated to bring it up; it was an abuse that, according to the PBS documentary *Freedom Riders*, served to "humiliate and terrorize female prisoners." The tactic worked. One of the last vestiges of privacy was ripped away as the women endured the painful and humiliating process of being on the receiving end of an invasive body search. Even at Parchman the prison administrators had the good sense to ensure that female guards conducted these searches, but that's where their sense ran out. Rather than being required to change gloves between prisoners, the female guards simply dipped their gloved hands into buckets of Lysol—a half-hearted attempt at hygiene, at best.

Mimi was spared this particular indignity ("they hadn't figured it out yet"), but she was still incarcerated when they did start to institute the vaginal searches, and she heard the results. "From our cells," Mimi tells me, "we could hear the women screaming."

═══

Of all the indignities the Freedom Riders endured while in prison— monotony, lack of exercise, and painful body searches, just to name a few— there was at least one violation in which the Riders got the better of the guards. "The mattress incident," Mimi called it. After several days of enduring the Riders' never-ending repertoire of freedom songs, the Parchman prison guards decided they'd had enough. The songs were too loud and powerful and did too much to lift the prisoners' morale. As a result the guards did their best to squelch the singing. Yet despite their demands that the prisoners knock off the racket, the guards were unable to silence the continual thrum of freedom songs. *If you don't stop with the singing*, the guards threatened, *then we'll take away your mattresses.*

Of course, the Riders refused to stop singing. In fact, Hank Thomas—who endured both the Anniston bus firebombing and a stretch at Parchman—even shoved his mattress against the bars, hollering, "Come get my mattress, I'll keep my soul." Making good on their threat, the Parchman guards removed the mattresses, forcing two of the three prisoners in each cell to sleep on steel box springs and the third to curl up on the concrete. Making matters worse, the air cooling system was set to its chilliest setting, creating an icy situation that made the nights all but unbearable.

"But," Mimi said proudly, "we survived." It's a mantra I heard again and again from the Freedom Riders. They did survive, with their souls intact. But that doesn't mean they didn't suffer.

=====

In the August issue of the *CORE-lator*, CORE National Director James Farmer wrote, "Jail at best is neither a romantic nor a pleasant place. Mississippi jails are no exception." Having spent forty days in Parchman, Farmer surely knew. And so did Mimi, who, after serving her own forty-day stint, was released back into the world unbroken. She and Judy Frieze were released together, and a wave of relief rushed through them as they exited the prison gates to spot Judy's parents waiting by their car. The Friezes drove Mimi north, reuniting her with her parents at the Feingold family's rental cabin in upstate New York.

I tried to wrap my head around the juxtaposition: how one night Mimi was sleeping on a Mississippi prison floor and the next in a bed in New York. So much of Mimi's story fascinates me, most of all her strength. I searched her mug shot for clues to her resiliency, and I was hardly surprised to find a grinning twenty-year-old staring back. "In the photo," I began, in my interview with her, "it almost looks like you're smiling. You're getting booked, and you're smiling. Do you remember why?"

"There are two reasons, and I remember them both very distinctly," Mimi said, then paused to reconsider. "Well, I guess three reasons."

The first was that she knew she was innocent of any crime. "With most mug shots, the people arrested know perfectly well they've done something awful. It's a grim situation. But this wasn't grim," she explained. "I wasn't a convict. I was a soldier."

The second reason is somewhat amusing. "If someone sticks a camera in your face, you smile. It was like getting your driver's license picture taken. They had this mark on the floor where you'd stand, and there was a camera behind the counter, and so I automatically smiled."

But it's her third reason for smiling that is most compelling, offering me the greatest insight into Mimi's strength. "Smiling fit with my way of digging the thing back into them," she declared. "There was no way that I was going to show them that I was anything other than a soldier for justice. I was not a victim, I was not a criminal, I was not scared of them. I was proud of what I'd done. I wasn't going to let them deny me that."

Upon hearing her explanation, I couldn't help but smile myself.

"I was young and idealistic," Mimi concluded, noting two essential characteristics that drove the movement forward. Despite the difficulties soon to come, that day in the Jackson City Jail, Mimi made a choice. She would not be a victim; she would not be scared. To prove it, she turned toward the camera and smiled.

Figure 5. Charles Person (left) and the author, March 2016.
Used by permission of Larrick Potvin.

4

Charles Person

Atlanta, Georgia

> *"My real wish in life is that at some point we could have a sit-down—a cup of coffee or a slice of pizza—with the people who beat us. I was five foot six and 126 pounds. For them to have that much venom toward people they have never met before—I'd like to have a sit-down and ask why."*

I had barely boarded the bus before wondering if I was making a terrible mistake. After all, what kind of professor dedicates his spring break to spending even more time with students? My kind, I suppose—although I was equally motivated to sign up for our university's civil rights pilgrimage by the prospect of meeting Charles Person. I knew only fragments of his story, but I was eager to learn more and to meet my first Freedom Rider face-to-face.

I arrived at my university's dormitories (the agreed-upon meeting place) a few minutes before three o'clock on a Friday afternoon in March. The campus was a ghost town; most of the students had already begun their weeklong ritual of hitting the beaches instead of the books. They deserved it—we all did. Yet I, along with eighty or so students and colleagues, had opted to spend our spring break differently. We hoped to further our education by logging miles—crisscrossing the South as part of a civil rights tour, our effort to move beyond the history books to live a bit of that history.

My own decision to join the ride was further buoyed by an aphorism first offered by Rabbi Hillel and later paraphrased by John Lewis (describing his own reasons for joining the Freedom Rides): "If not us, then who? If not now, then when?" The difference, of course, is that when John Lewis boarded the bus he risked his life, whereas when I boarded all these years later, all I was sacrificing was spring break and a few days with my family.

This trip would be the longest I had ever been away from my wife and my children, and even though my wife had a hard time giving me too much sympathy ("Yeah," she said dryly, "a weeklong vacation sounds rough"), it was, in fact, going to be a little rough. I knew I would miss them a lot. I figured my one-year-old daughter would quickly replace me with a bit of Big Bird, but my four-year-old son might take my absence harder, or at least notice that I was no longer there.

They accompanied me to the dormitories for my send-off. "Do you want to see where Daddy's going to be for the next nine days?" my wife asked the children. They did, and my son bounded up the bus steps while my daughter took her place in the crook of her mother's arm. From my place on the curb, I watched the students gather: a flock of backpacked brethren, each of whom was anxious to secure prime seating on our soon-to-be home on wheels.

I stayed quiet, eavesdropping on the low lull of conversations taking place around me. *What dorm are you in? What's your major? You heard the new Beyoncé song?* Dormless and majorless with but a cursory knowledge of the latest Beyoncé song, I tried to make myself invisible. Already I was an outsider, which I knew would make things tricky if I was trying to get these students to open up to me. That indeed was one of my two goals for the trip. I wanted to capture the perspectives and insights of my students, some of whom were learning about civil rights for the first time. I wanted to see what they saw, hear what they said, and better understand what was likely to seem anachronistic to some of them: the notion that one's skin color can dictate so many aspects of one's life. I also couldn't help but wonder about the students' take on our country's current racial climate, as well as what lessons they thought we might glean from the past and incorporate into the present.

My second goal was a bit more tangible. This was my scouting mission, my effort to begin piecing together an itinerary for my return trip to the South, scheduled for mid-May. I had decided that to understand the Freedom Rides more fully, I needed to retrace portions of the original route myself. And that is precisely what I intended to do once I had decided which portions to retrace.

As the Beyoncé talk wound down, my son leaped from the bus and rushed toward me, smiling.

"How was it?" I asked.

"There was a bathroom!" he replied.

"A bathroom?"

"A bathroom!"

"Wow," I said, with a low whistle. "The future has arrived."

"Okay," someone shouted, interrupting our toilet talk, "time to load up." The students did as they were instructed. But before I boarded I took another moment to smother the kids with hugs, making promises of extravagant souvenirs that I knew my wallet wouldn't make good on.

"Good luck," I said, hugging my wife.

"Enjoy your vacation," she joked.

"Hey, now I've got to keep an eye on eighty kids," I protested, nodding toward the students. "You've only got to worry about two."

She scoffed, and I smiled; both of us were fully aware that my math didn't quite add up. My son began his shoulder-slumped retreat toward the minivan, while my daughter—still in the crook of her mother's arm—offered me a wobbly wave. A moment later they were buckled into their car seats, and two moments later they were gone. Swallowing the lump in my throat, I turned to the nearest crowd of college students, all of whom witnessed our farewell. "Well," I joked, hiding the sadness in my voice, "I guess you're my children now." They confirmed it by rolling their eyes.

=====

Fifty-five years earlier and eight hundred miles away in the nation's capital, another group of students and citizens once boarded buses. They too left their loved ones behind, bidding farewell to family and friends with no guarantee of a reunion.

Among the CORE Freedom Riders was eighteen-year-old Charles Person, the youngest of the original Freedom Riders. Born in Atlanta in September 1942, Charles eventually found himself to be passionate about math and science, and in the fall of 1960 this passion drove him to enroll at Morehouse College, where he hoped to study nuclear physics. The school wasn't his first choice, but his options were limited. The all-white Georgia Institute of Technology had, of course, denied his application, whereas the Massachusetts Institute of Technology had accepted him—but it offered no scholarships, thereby denying him the opportunity by other means.

During his senior year at David T. Howard High School, Charles became a member of the local NAACP's Youth Council, and by the time he entered Morehouse he was already well versed in the strategies and goals of the civil rights movement. Throughout his freshman year his commitment to the cause continued to grow, and his first demonstration took place at a segregated lunch counter in Atlanta in early 1961. Charles was promptly arrested, which only emboldened him. If necessary, he decided, he would put his goal of becoming a nuclear physicist on hold to further commit himself to the movement.

In the spring of 1961, as James Farmer and the rest of the CORE leadership team began scouting for a Freedom Rider from Atlanta, Charles's name was suggested. Not only was he committed, he was also tested. And he possessed what for CORE was probably the most important attribute of all: an ability to remain nonviolent even in the most heated situations. He had proved this during his lunch-counter sit-ins.

Decades after the completion of the Freedom Rides, Charles learned that he had yet another advantage over other equally eligible activists on every stool at every lunch counter: "I was squeaky clean," he explained. "I hadn't lived long enough to have anything in my background." He'd been arrested, but what civil rights activist hadn't? And in the 1960s, a civil rights–inspired arrest was akin to a merit badge. More important to CORE was how he had handled his arrests. There was little question within the CORE leadership team that eighteen-year-old Charles Person possessed the experience, the intelligence, and the cool-headedness necessary for the journey. It was only a matter of getting him to take his seat on the bus.

═══

Half an hour into our ride, a student coordinator spoke into the bus microphone. "Oka-a-ay," she called, the enthusiasm rising in her voice, "time for an icebreaker!" Our instructions were clear. Those of us in the aisle seats were to rotate through the empty seats directly in front of us, thereby giving us a chance to interact with as many other passengers as possible. At each seat stop we would be asked a question, which we were to mull over together before moving on to the next seat. Sounds simple enough, I thought. And it would have been, if the questions had been softballs—but they weren't, always.

A few questions in, the student coordinator peered down at her paper and read, "Describe a time when you felt discriminated against." It was a bit of a stumper for a straight white man such as myself. All around me, however, were people who had little trouble coming up with an answer. Although our group was primarily white, it was also primarily female. A few African American and Hmong students were also on board, and there were several students from places such as China, Malaysia, Malawi, India, Mexico, and Latvia.

But mostly we were white, so when we got to the discrimination question,

I was, as the probabilities assured, sitting by another white person. My seat-mate, a young woman, mulled over the question alongside me. Eventually we settled on answers that we both admitted were less about discrimination than the slight anxiety we had occasionally felt when we ourselves were in the minority. Neither of us was thrilled with our answers, which were mostly nonanswers and further proof of the privilege we shared.

How astonishing, I thought, that for me discrimination still remains mostly a hypothetical, a situation I have witnessed but rarely faced. It was all the more troubling given that so many face it so often, and for some it never ends. I was just beginning to mull this over when the icebreaker propelled us on—eventually circling me back to the seat directly behind my original seat.

"Bee-ja-a-ay!" exclaimed D'Karlos Craig, the twenty-four-year-old African American student seated beside me. "What's going on?" He shook my hand and gave me a smooth smile. I had met D'Karlos a few weeks earlier, during a pretrip orientation meeting in which I had shared a bit about my project with the students. He had expressed interest from the start, agreeing to help me see the world through his eyes and help me understand discrimination as something more than hypothetical.

"Okay," the student coordinator continued, reading off the final question. "If you could get rid of one thing in the world, what would it be?" Clearly the time for softball questions was over. "Hmm," D'Karlos said, squinting in deep concentration while peering out the window. "One thing I'd get rid of . . ."

I kept my answer light, joking that I'd probably rid the world of composition class. His eyes widened. This admission—coming from an English professor, no less!—must have surely seemed like blasphemy. "I mean, I don't mind the class," I quickly backpedaled, "but the thought of teaching it again and again until my dying day, well, that's just a lot of composition class. A lot of comma splices, you know?"

D'Karlos laughed. "I hear ya," he said.

"What about you?" I asked.

"Well, for me," he replied, scratching his chin, "I'd probably just rid the world of hunger."

So much for keeping it light, I thought.

"There's just so much wealth out there," he continued, "and I think we just got to do a better job of spreading that wealth around in such a way that people don't have to go hungry."

I was embarrassed. *Composition class? Really, Hollars?*

Sensing my embarrassment, D'Karlos came to my rescue. "Oh, and maybe GE courses, too," he said with a grin, referring to the mandatory general education classes that are nearly as popular as composition.

I smiled. "Nah," I said, returning to my original seat, "I think you got it right the first time."

═══

Charles Person never saw a social justice fight he didn't like. Although his life as a demonstrator began with the civil rights movement, he continued to tackle other issues as well, from poverty to education to Native American rights. "Once you get involved in social justice, you can't stop," he told me later. For him demonstrating was akin to breathing; it was what one did to survive.

After his time on the Freedom Rides, his mother began to grow nervous about the potential for retribution. She believed that his public civil rights efforts made him a clear target for vigilante justice, and in an attempt to alleviate her fears she suggested that her son join the army. He joined the US Marine Corps instead, and eventually fought in Vietnam. The irony was hardly lost on me: for a black man in America in the 1960s, it seemed safer to be a soldier stationed overseas than a citizen in his own country. (It wasn't however: he has endured the effects of Agent Orange for the rest of his life.)

These days, at age seventy-three, Charles has mostly turned his attention to inspiring the next generation of social justice foot soldiers. His unflagging faith in students, in particular, is noteworthy—a reminder to people like me, who interact with eighteen-year-olds daily, that eighteen-year-olds possess the power to change the world.

Charles is proof. At eighteen he boarded a Freedom Rides bus. Fifty-five years later, his journey continues.

═══

The following day the college students and I paid the price for our night spent on the bus. After covering over a thousand miles in twenty hours, we emerged from the bus exhausted, stumbling down its stairs into a beautiful Atlanta afternoon. This city—the birthplace of both Dr. King and Charles Person—was our first stop. For much of the afternoon our attention was focused solely on King, a name synonymous with the civil rights movement. We divided into groups, then began walking up and down Auburn

Avenue, a historic black neighborhood that contains the King Center, the Ebenezer Baptist Church, and King's birth home: a yellow two-story house with brown shutters, complete with a wide veranda and a porch swing rocking gently in the wind. Once deemed the "richest Negro street in the world," today Auburn Avenue is a National Historical Landmark, and the flocks of tourists certainly make it feel like one.

The historical magnitude of the street had barely sunk in before we were whisked to our next stop: the Center for Civil and Human Rights, a museum in Atlanta's Pemberton Place. As we trudged toward the museum I overheard the sleepy-eyed students calling dibs on showers and beds, even though these luxuries were still a few hours away. For now our job was to be dutiful museumgoers: to look at exhibits, read placards, nod thoughtfully, and soak in all the knowledge we could. I was as bedraggled as the others, and as I meandered around the floors I found it harder and harder to nod without nodding off. And forget about the placards—my sleepy eyes could only handle so much.

On the museum's second floor I spotted a line of people patiently waiting for something. Even though I didn't know what that something was, the line seemed like a great opportunity to lean against the wall for a while. So I did, closing my eyes for a moment while in search of my second wind. I never found it, but what I did find, ten minutes later, was myself at the front of the line. At that point a woman hastily ushered me to a stool alongside three others at a replica 1960s-era lunch counter. I did as I was told, passing a sign that warned me that the experience I was about to undertake "may be too graphic for children under 10 years old." Uh-oh, I thought. What have I gotten myself into?

The woman told me to place the earphones on my head and my hands on the counter. It was an order, not a suggestion. So I followed the orders, wholly unaware of what was coming. At first all I heard was silence, but soon that silence was interrupted by a hissing in my ear. Then the hissing was interrupted by another sound—shattering glass—directly followed by a male voice, then several male voices, and then several more male voices shifting from my left ear to my right. I was trapped in their surround sound, and although the men weren't present, I felt strangely claustrophobic by the closeness of their voices.

"Git up, git up, boy," one voice whispered. "Git up! I'm going to take this fork and—" I felt a jolt in my stool. "Git up! Git up!" cried another. "Git up! Git up!" There was more shattering glass, more hissing, and then suddenly the enactment was so vivid that I swore I could feel the oppressors' spittle in my ear.

The lunch-counter simulation lasted less than two minutes, yet each passing second, which ticked off on a clock directly in front of me, felt endless. All I wanted was for it to be over, and when it finally was, I couldn't pull the headphones from my ears fast enough. Suddenly I had been reminded that I was a white man in 2016. I pushed myself weakly from the stool so the next person could have a turn, but I didn't leave the lunch-counter area. Instead I lingered just a few feet behind it, curious to watch the physical reactions of the people now sitting on the stools: the way their back muscles tightened and constricted, the way they sighed and scratched their nails on the counter.

The experience felt so real to me that the word "simulation" seems inaccurate. "Git up, boy, git up!" I heard the echoes of that long after I had left that lunch counter, that museum, and even that state. "Git up, boy!" And in the moment after my turn on the stool, I asked myself, Would I have gotten up?

I pondered this question again while lifting an audio device from an adjacent bus replica coated with Freedom Rider portraits. I placed the device to my ear and listened as one Freedom Rider after another recounted his or her story. But as I listened, my eyes drifted back toward that lunch counter, where I spotted D'Karlos taking his turn on the stool. I watched as he placed the headphones over his ears, and I studied him for some reaction. But his body offered no clues. Two minutes later, once it was over, he rose and peered out at the world. He saw me and wandered my way.

"Well," I asked, "how was it?"

"Too much information," he sighed, shaking his head. "Too much information."

The next day we were destined to get even more of it.

=====

We arrived at the Georgia Tech Student Center a little before nine o'clock in the morning and descended to the lower level to meet Charles Person. In the past eighteen hours we had toured museums, churches, and historical homes, but we had yet to meet any civil rights activists firsthand. So this was the moment we'd been waiting for.

I, the overenthusiastic professor, took a seat front-row center—the best seat in the house. The students forgave me for my indulgence. After twenty hours on the bus together, they all knew—probably more than they *needed* to know—just how anxious I was to have my first face-to-face encounter with a Freedom Rider.

I had been reading about Charles for months, learning his story one detail at a time. But in all that time, what I wanted most was to meet him and hear his story through his own words, unfiltered. That is exactly what I prepared for as I watched Charles grip his walker while making his way to the front of the room. "I'm sorry I'm late," he called out, as his wife trailed just a few steps behind him. "We've been trying for some time to find our way in." The building is a bit of a maze, and given his reliance on a walker, I could imagine that accessibility might have proved challenging as well. Upon reaching the front of the room, Charles transformed his walker into a seat, settling in for the long conversation ahead. He was decked out in a black tuxedo adorned with military medals, an outfit that put our own Sunday best to shame.

Reaching for the mic, Charles asked, "Can someone here start us off with a hymn?"

Oh no, I thought, immediately regretting my prime real estate in the center of the front row. Suddenly I was a hymn-singing target, and since I don't know a hymn from a Gregorian chant, I shrunk down in my seat.

"Anyone?" Charles asked again, and I shrunk lower. "No one?" he asked once more. By the grace of God, an elementary school music teacher had accompanied us on our trip, and after a bit of coaxing she agreed to sing a hymn. "How about 'Precious Lord'?" Charles suggested.

"Pick another," the music teacher said, unfamiliar with the words. Charles picked another. "Umm, pick another," the teacher repeated, red-faced. The room laughed.

"How about this," Charles suggested, "how about we all sing 'The Battle Hymn of the Republic'?" Now he was speaking our language, and even though we mostly only knew the refrain, upon reaching it we belted it out with enough gusto to make up for all the verses we had forgotten. "His **truth** is marching **on!**"

"All right, then." Charles smiled at the song's conclusion. "Now we can begin." He cleared his throat, peered down at his hands, and blanketed us in a rare moment of silence. "I know it's difficult to talk about race for a number of reasons," he began. "But that's what we're going to do here." He set the tone by explaining that he and Hank Thomas (by 2016 the only two survivors among the original CORE Freedom Rides) held no grudge against those who had physically harmed them on Mother's Day 1961. "My real wish in life," he said, "is that at some point we could have a sit-down—a cup of coffee or a slice of pizza—with the people who beat us."

It was hard for me to imagine that people could hate one another so intensely based on skin color alone. It shouldn't be. But that precedent ran deep. "I was five foot six and 126 pounds," Charles continued. "For them to have that much venom toward people they have never met before—I'd like to have a sit-down and ask why."

Much of Charles's talk centered on one question, which I had first considered after speaking with Jim Zwerg several months earlier. "What," Charles challenged us, "would you get on the bus for?" It was the kind of soul-probing question that kept me up at night, and even though it was hypothetical, it could turn real in an instant. It was a question that demanded introspection and reflection—a good hard look at oneself in the mirror. It was a question that revealed my own reticence to act, reminding me of just how few causes I would be willing to lay down my life for. I imagine I'm not alone.

"We were very young, very optimistic," Charles said, his eyes glazing over as he summoned the past. "Today," he quipped, snapping back to the present, "I'm not so young. But I'm still optimistic." In addition to being young and optimistic, Charles admitted, perhaps he was also a little naive. "We figured the worst that would happen to us was someone might throw ketchup on us, or sugar, or spit on us," he explained. "Little did we know it could get worse."

On the morning of Mother's Day, May 14, 1961, eighteen-year-old Charles joined his fellow Freedom Riders at the Trailways station in Atlanta. Not far away, a second group assembled at the Greyhound station. Both buses were bound for Birmingham, but only one would make it there by the end of the day.

The Greyhound bus left an hour ahead of the Trailways bus and made its way into Alabama around lunchtime. Among the Greyhound riders sat a pair of undercover Alabama State highway patrolmen, Corporals Ell Cowling and Harry Sims, who were assigned to blend in with the other non-Freedom Rider passengers. They had been dispatched for intelligence-gathering purposes, but within hours the circumstances would force them to take a more active role.

As Charles and his fellow Trailways riders barreled toward Birmingham, nineteen-year-old Hank Thomas and his crew ran into trouble at the Greyhound station in Anniston. Of the many Freedom Riders on the Greyhound bus that day, Hank delivers the best rendition of how he and the others watched as their bus pulled into the station only to find themselves suddenly at the center of a mob.

It was the Freedom Riders' first real threat of mass violence, and even though they had prepared for it, preparation was not enough. The attackers came bearing pipes, chains, and brass knuckles, and for twenty minutes or so they pounded the bus as if trying to crack it wide open. Hank and the other riders looked down from their windows, watching as the faces in the mob twisted with rage as the attackers hurled one insult after another.

Quietly and powerlessly the Riders awaited their fate, which at that moment remained uncertain. The uncertainty subsided when the police arrived on the scene, motioning the bus back onto the highway and providing the riders with temporary relief. As the bus left the station, the riders glanced back to find themselves trailed by a parade of overflowing cars and trucks. As the riders viewed the changing ground situation, one thing became abundantly clear to them: they would never outrun their pursuers. Thanks to a few carefully placed punctures courtesy of the mob, the bus's tires were rapidly deflating. Making matters worse, a few of the cars had also begun forcing the bus to the side of the road.

The bus eventually shuddered to a halt across from Forsyth and Son Grocery Store. Cowling and Sims rushed toward the front to pin the doors closed and keep out the attackers. Within twenty minutes, however, the attackers found a way to bypass the door, breaking a window and tossing inside a Molotov cocktail–style firebomb. As the smoke increased, Cowling and Sims's door-holding strategy suddenly reversed. Now they were desperate to push the doors open, but the mob prevented this. "Burn them niggers alive!" the mob hollered. A carnival atmosphere had developed around them.

"It was at that point that I thought that I was going to die," Hank later remarked, "and it was a question of deciding which way I wanted to die." The tall muscular African American man weighed two equally damning options. He could push his way through and take his chances with the weapon-wielding mob, or he could resign himself to the smoke and the flames billowing around him. "In those few seconds I thought, 'Well, maybe the best way to die is on the bus, and since it's a great deal of smoke, if I just breathed in heavily of the smoke, then I would pass out,' and that's truly what I thought."

But Hank's body refused to succumb. As his lungs filled with smoke, his body revolted and hurled itself toward the bus doors, which were still blocked by a sea of angry white faces. As the air thinned, a fuel tank suddenly erupted; the blast was so deafening that even the attackers abandoned their posts to take cover. The Freedom Riders seized the opportunity to escape, but they didn't get far. In the tall grass surrounding the bus, the mob continued its fight—corralling the Riders as close to the flames as possible. With the heat pressing against their backs, the Riders found themselves in a dilemma quite similar to the one Hank had just faced: Which fate was worse, the fire or the mob? In the confusion a few Riders began to escape unnoticed, but as Hank stumbled from the burning bus, a white man spotted him.

"Are you all right, boy?" the man asked. When Hank confirmed that he was, the man bludgeoned him with a baseball bat, ensuring that he was no longer "all right."

Meanwhile, from her place at the edge of her father's store, twelve-year-old Janie Forsyth watched. The buck-toothed, brown-eyed white girl had witnessed the chaos from the start, staring wide-eyed as the Greyhound bus lurched to a halt just beyond the store. She watched too as the bus filled with flames and the Riders began tumbling onto the grass. Overcome by a desire to do something, anything, she reached for a nearby pail and began filling it with water. She ran back and forth with her sloshing pail between the store and the sputtering Riders, offering as much water to them as she could. Her efforts, however modest, were nothing short of heroic. After all, her actions were in open defiance of the mob that surrounded her. The Riders watched as the young girl wore a path through the grass, hustling to help those in need.

To Janie, the collision of events that brought the Riders to her father's store was irrelevant. Her actions weren't meant to be political, cultural, or an affront to racial protocol. She simply reacted as a human being should: people were in trouble, and she was in a position to help. Her thin arms held the pail out to Hank Thomas, who peered up at her white face and at last saw someone who wasn't there to harm him.

———

Meanwhile, back on the other bus, Charles Person and the other Trailways riders peered nervously out the windows as they crossed the state line. Days later—in the aftermath of everything soon to come—Charles would tell a *Time* magazine reporter that as they left Georgia and entered Alabama he felt a visceral change. "The atmosphere," Charles explained, "was tense."

From his place in the front left seat, he heard a white passenger confirm this observation. "You niggers had it good in Georgia," the man hissed, "but you're in Alabama now."

"I didn't think much about it, because he was getting off the bus," Charles explained as we sat at rapt attention in our seats in the Georgia Tech Student Center. "But then he got some of his friends together. I would see him a few hours later in Birmingham." In fact, Klansmen had been traveling on the Trailways bus since Atlanta and had spent much of the journey verbally harassing them.

After a brief stop at the Anniston station, the bus driver reboarded and informed the Riders of the fate of their friends on the Greyhound bus. "We have received word that a bus has been burned to the ground," the driver said, "and passengers are being carried to the hospital in carloads." Charles tried to remain calm, but his empathy for the Greyhound Riders soon turned to fear for his own safety. Before the bus had left the Anniston station, eight white men climbed aboard and demanded that the black Riders move to the back.

After threats failed to pry the Riders from their seats, the hoodlums turned violent, targeting the two nearest African Americans—Charles and a man named Herman Harris—both of whom endured a flurry of blows as they were shoved toward the back of the bus. "We were about halfway back when [James] Peck and [Walter] Bergman came to help," Charles explained. Woefully outnumbered, however, the white Riders had little to defend themselves with but their bodies.

From his place a few seats away, *Jet* reporter Simeon Booker recounted the scene in full. "In a second," Booker wrote, "the white toughs were raining blows on every Negro in the front section. The attack was savage, flecked with obscene utterances." And as Booker confirmed, Peck and Bergman's efforts to ease the tension only created the opposite effect. "The ruffians transferred their fury to the whites," Booker wrote. "A right [hook] lifted slender-as-a-reed Peck over two seats and dropped him into the aisle. Bergman was battered into semiconsciousness, and as he lay in the aisle, one of the whites jumped up and down on his chest with his feet."

Riders of both races did their best to protect themselves, but their efforts proved only moderately successful. After all, they were trapped on a moving bus with nowhere to run or hide. "Peck was a bleeder," Charles remembered, referring to the forty-six-year-old white man who was the only Freedom

Rider who had participated in the Journey of Reconciliation as well. "His blood," Charles continued, "coated the floor and made it slippery as they pushed us back."

Beaten and semiconscious, the assaulted Riders lay in the bus's back seats as the driver took an alternative route to Birmingham. The Klansmen kept close watch from their place in the center of the bus, ensuring that no Riders dared breach the barrier they had established. The Riders didn't. Thus, for the next two hours, the beaten Riders and the bloodthirsty Klansmen maintained a steely-eyed stalemate, the latter hurling threats while the former endured them in silence.

When at last the bus arrived at the Trailways terminal, Charles Person and James Peck, both beaten and bloodied, led their fellow Riders into the waiting room. They had hardly made it inside before the assault resumed, with the number of assailants vastly multiplied. "There was this entire wall of men coming toward us," Charles recalled. "They had bats and pipes. Some [Riders] said they saw the butts of guns hanging out."

Peck, a bit smaller and older than Charles, was knocked to the ground within seconds. Charles managed to endure the blows a bit longer, but soon he too fell to the floor, shielding his body as well as he could while he was being pummeled. "It was the most terrible mob action I have ever witnessed," Booker wrote. "An explosion of race hate and prejudice rocked the Magic City terminal. I watched as Peck, blood dried on his face, and Charles Person trudged down the ramp toward the main waiting room through a row of the meanest-looking whites." The others followed, entering the proverbial lion's den despite knowing full well what awaited them.

Booker later described the scene in graphic detail: how the mob sealed the terminal exits, then proceeded to beat the Riders mercilessly, and how the Klansmen's blows tore first into Charles, then into James Peck, and then anyone else within arm's reach. Eventually Charles escaped, but, as Booker reported, not everyone was so lucky. The forty-two-year-old black reporter watched in horror as Peck lay "prostrate on the floor" and as a bloody-faced Walter Bergman "crawl[ed] on hands and knees trying to find a door."

=====

It's easy to see the Mother's Day violence as little more than another example of a white southern mob set aflame. But the beatings and bus firebombing that occurred on May 14, 1961, were in fact watershed moments for the movement, prompting writer David Halberstam to deem it "the day the

Rubicon was crossed. . . . This was no minor, little venture into sampling hamburgers in different bus stations," he wrote. "This, instead, was a frontal assault on the very nature of the beast of segregation, in the place where it was most powerful."

Upon escaping the bus terminal, Charles Person rushed to the street, where he frantically boarded a city bus that transported him two blocks to the other side of the railroad tracks. When onlookers informed him that his head was bleeding, he began searching for a doctor, but all the white doctors refused to treat him. Finally Charles was driven to a church, where a nurse bandaged his head to stop the bleeding. "I had a large knot on the base of my skull," Charles told us, pointing to the back of his head. "I was sure I had some razor blade in there or something, but an MRI showed it was just drainage at the base of the skull." For thirty-five years he lived with that knot, a daily reminder of the violence wrought upon him on that fateful day. It wasn't until 1996 that he finally had the knot removed.

After being treated, many of the Freedom Riders joined Charles at Reverend Fred Shuttlesworth's Bethel Baptist Church the same night. Shuttlesworth, one of Birmingham's most prominent civil rights leaders, stood before his church, beaming. "This is the greatest thing that has ever happened to Alabama," he declared from the pulpit, "and it has been good for the nation. It was a wonderful thing to see these young students—Negro and white—come, even after the mobs and the bus burning. When white and black men are willing to be beaten up together, it is a sure sign they will soon walk together as brothers."

It seemed a peculiar moment for a victory speech, given the horrors the Freedom Riders had endured that day. Yet Shuttlesworth seemed to see the larger picture. Even though the Riders' nonviolent strategy may have made it seem that they were losing the physical battle, they were in fact winning the public relations war. Each photo had the power to change hearts and minds, and in the coming hours, as Americans turned on their televisions and opened their newspapers, many throughout the nation would see—in graphic detail—just how horrific the beatings and bombing had been. This was visual proof that both black and white people were being injured indiscriminately, a confirmation for many Americans that what had once seemed to be a black problem was actually a national problem.

The following day, when no bus driver would agree to take them to their final destination of New Orleans, the Riders traded in the buses for a plane and took to the skies instead. One way or another, they would make it to the sea, as Mahatma Gandhi had during his Salt March thirty-one years earlier while protesting British rule. Yet shortly after boarding their plane at the Birmingham airport, a bomb threat that required clearing the plane made it evident to the Riders that the sky could be as dangerous as the road. Nonetheless, with some assistance from John Seigenthaler of the Justice Department, the Riders reboarded the plane and flew without incident.

From his window seat, eighteen-year-old Charles peered down at the America waiting for him far below. And despite all that he had endured that day, he was still proud of what he saw. As imperfect as the country was, he knew he could make it better.

═══

As our conversation at Georgia Tech wound down, Charles turned his attention to his current fight: recruiting the next generation for the battles that lay ahead. "It's *your* turn," he challenged, allowing the moment to linger. "It was easy for us to get on the bus, but now it's up to you. Change," he continued, "begins with young people. Always has, always will."

He paused, meeting the eyes of the students who surrounded me. "*You* can change the world," he stated simply. "You must realize this. Who would have thought in 1961 that our motley crew could make a difference? When I talk to young people, I tell them this. I say, 'When you get up in the morning and brush your teeth and your hair, look in the mirror and say, "I can change the world." When you do this enough you'll believe it.'"

Half an hour later, after a flurry of handshakes and photographs and our exit from the room, I still feared there was a good chance that we would forget Charles's call for action—that instead of confronting the challenges that lay ahead, we would opt for the easier road: resigning ourselves to the world we have rather than strive toward the one we hope to have.

Soon we were back on the bus to continue to our next destination. But we were different now: quieter, more contemplative, a bit more willing to act. "What did you think?" I asked D'Karlos as he slipped his headphones over his ears.

"Man," he said, smiling, "too much information."

D'Karlos's repeated phrasing triggered the threats I had heard during the lunch-counter simulation the previous day. "Git up, boy, git up!" When Charles first heard those words, it was no simulation, it was real life. I stared out the window as our ride rolled on. And I asked myself, Would I have gotten up?

PART II

The Road Ahead

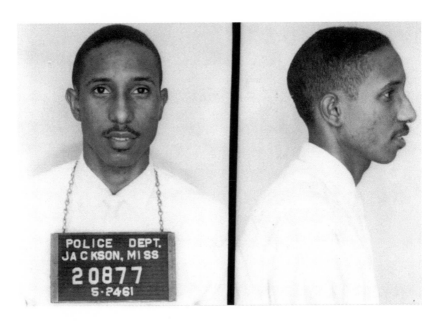

Figure 6. Bernard LaFayette Jr., mug shot, May 24, 1961.

Mississippi State Sovereignty Commission, "Mississippi State Sovereignty Commission Photograph," May 24, 1961, SCRID# 2-55-2-68-1-1-1ph, Series 2515: Mississippi State Sovereignty Commission Records, 1994–2006, Mississippi Department of Archives and History, February 20, 2017, http://mdah.ms.gov/arrec/digital_archives/sovcom/photo.php?display=item&oid=71.

5

Bernard LaFayette Jr.

Tampa, Florida

"For me there was no question about whether we were going to continue the Ride. If those guys almost got killed and were ready to continue, I was convinced the rest of us should, too."

From the baggage claim at the Montgomery Regional Airport, I placed the call. One ring, two rings, three.

"Hello?"

"Dr. LaFayette?" I asked.

"Yes?"

I reintroduced myself, or tried to.

"Oh, it's you again," Bernard LaFayette Jr. said with a chuckle. "You sure are persistent."

"It's just that I've come a long way," I explained. "And I really don't want to miss out on the chance to talk with you."

"Oh, you won't," he promised. "I'm in a meeting now, but let's meet at the museum later this afternoon. Can you meet me there? We'll all be there."

We'll all be there. At the mere prospect, a grin spread wide across my face. "That'll be perfect," I agreed. "I look forward to seeing you all soon." My "you all" referred to the Freedom Riders, twenty or so of whom have descended upon Montgomery for the fifty-fifth anniversary of the Freedom Rides.

Although meeting Freedom Riders en masse was never part of my original plan, I knew to take the detour when I saw it. And so, rather than retrace the Freedom Riders' routes as intended, I did what any good writer does: revised heavily. I scrapped the plan, changed the plane ticket, and extended my stay at Montgomery's Red Roof Inn. Rather than having to employ my needle-in-a-haystack approach to finding Freedom Riders, I was fortunate enough to have them come to me—or at least come together, thereby making it easier for me to interact with at least a dozen Riders all at once.

Now it was just a matter of getting myself to Montgomery's Freedom Rides Museum: the site of the former Greyhound station where, fifty-five years ago on this day, Bernard LaFayette and so many others were beaten at the hands of a mob.

Exiting the baggage claim area, I hustled to the rental car lot, where, after an extensive search, I found a nondescript four-door sedan—my chariot for the next nine days. Soon it would take me on my five-hundred-mile journey from Montgomery to Anniston, from Birmingham to Jackson, and, if all went as planned, to Parchman Farm—the final stop for most of the Freedom Riders as well.

I typed "Freedom Rides Museum" into my GPS and was told that my destination was nine miles away. I buckled up, started the car, and at last began my ride. I've got this, I thought, as I made a right turn out of the lot. The funny thing was, I believed I did. What could possibly go wrong, after all? It was just a short little ride through the South.

———

Fifty-five years earlier, Bernard LaFayette learned precisely all that could possibly go wrong during a "short little ride through the South." Of course, he had been aware of the country's racial problems long before he was beaten at the Montgomery Greyhound station on May 20, 1961.

Born in 1940 in Tampa, Florida, Bernard had his first glimpse of racism just a few years later while accompanying his grandmother on a trolley ride through the city. The seven-year-old watched as his grandmother inserted her coins into the receptacle at the front of the trolley car, then—as custom dictated—exited and attempted to reboard through the trolley's back door. However, in this instance she stumbled and fell before reboarding, and young Bernard watched in disbelief as the trolley car left without them. "I felt like a sword cut me in half," Bernard later described in his book, *In Peace and Freedom*, "and I vowed that I would do something about this problem one day."

In the fall of 1958 Bernard enrolled in Nashville's American Baptist Theological Seminary. There he met fellow students John Lewis and James Bevel, as well as a host of other socially conscious young African American students, all of whom would become allies in their shared fight for civil rights. That fall Bernard and others began attending nonviolence workshops led by the expert of the era: James Lawson, a Vanderbilt divinity student whose activism would lead to his expulsion. Despite this personal setback, Lawson would continue his training sessions, which became legendary—not only because of their effectiveness but also because of Lawson's unconventional role-playing methods. Under Lawson's guidance, the students were often forced to play the parts of both the vitriol-spewing segregationists and the targets of such remarks. Though emotionally challenging, Lawson's training paid off, and the nonviolent tactics he taught were destined to become one of the movement's most powerful weapons. Bernard wielded this weapon often.

Throughout the 1960s Bernard's disciplined approach to nonviolence catapulted him into various roles within the movement: Freedom Rider, director of the voting project in Alabama, national coordinator for the Poor People's Campaign, and program administrator for the Southern Christian Leadership Conference (Dr. King's organization). Over the years he grew close to Dr. King and worked with him often. After his mentor's assassination, however, Bernard slowed down his activism and recommitted himself to his education, earning a doctorate from Harvard University in 1974. For the next two decades Dr. LaFayette held positions at several universities, including president of his alma mater, the American Baptist Theological Seminary, and dean of the graduate school at Alabama State University in Montgomery. Despite living in Montgomery for years, he rarely found reason to return to the Greyhound station, the haunting locale where Freedom Riders' blood once pooled in the streets.

Today the former Greyhound station has mostly shaken its dark legacy. In 2011, to mark the fiftieth anniversary of the Freedom Rides, the space was reappropriated to become the Freedom Rides Museum. Except for the addition of a few informational placards and the removal of a "coloreds-only" entrance, the exterior now looks mostly as it did in 1961: a squat, brick, one-story structure complete with a vertical Greyhound sign directly above the main entrance.

I arrived shortly before Bernard and the other Freedom Riders returned from their meeting, and between browsing the exhibits I introduced myself to Dorothy Walker, the museum's newly installed director. Though born in the post–civil rights era, Dorothy, a native Alabamian, is no stranger to civil rights. Her relatives were involved in the voters' rights movement in Selma, which is why, she told me, she takes so much pride in her current position: it gives her the chance to preserve other people's stories.

Since the Freedom Riders' anniversary activities had begun the previous day, I knew I had some catching up to do. "How's it been so far?" I asked Dorothy. "How are the Riders?"

"Just amazing," she replied, beaming. "Last night I hung out with them at their hotel lobby, and let me tell you, they were getting down. Dancing, singing, telling all the old tales."

"Ah, geez," I said. "I can't believe I missed that. Think they'll do it again tonight?"

"Maybe," she said, smiling. "I hope."

In anticipation of their arrival I positioned myself on the museum's front steps. My body thrummed with excitement, although I was also a little afraid. It's one thing to study people's lives from afar, but it's quite another to actually meet the people you've been studying. The rewards are greater this way, but so are the risks. What if I said the wrong thing, did the wrong thing, or came off like some kind of deranged fan? All these scenarios were within the realm of possibility, but they were risks I was willing to take. The upside was simply too great to overlook. After all, within a few minutes I would be meeting several of my heroes, people whose stories I had been sharing for months to anyone willing to listen.

I took a breath, steadied my nerves, and watched as a short motorcade descended upon the Greyhound station, much as it had on this very day fifty-five years before. Only this time there were no buses, just vans and cars, and this time the Riders were more than half a century older. The Freedom Riders disembarked with the assistance of canes, walkers, and a few steady-handed volunteers. Time ensured that they had changed physically, but their spirits remained wholly intact. As the doors swung open, I was greeted by a crowd of smiling septuagenarians, all of whom, by the looks of things, appeared nearly as giddy as I was.

In an effort to be useful, I positioned myself as the museum's doorman, holding the glass door wide open as the Riders climbed the three or so steps leading into the former bus station. The Riders' processional lasted for several minutes as they nodded, waved, and posed for photographs with the dozen or so admirers waiting inside.

I recognized some of the Riders from their mug shots, although their name tags certainly assisted me in my identifications. However, I needed no name tag to identify the dapperly dressed Bernard LaFayette, who flashed me a brief smile before straightening his suit coat, adjusting his bowler hat, and slipping inside with the rest. I watched as he made his way toward a photo collage of Freedom Riders' mug shots on the right side of the museum, and within moments I found myself drifting toward him, joining the others who had gathered to watch him scan those faces now frozen in time.

He studied their youthful expressions one after another. They seemed to offer insight into the Riders' various motivations: indignation, frustration, and hope. Upon reaching the final photo he turned to the seventy-eight-year-old female Freedom Rider standing directly to his left. "You remember when we were in Hinds County Jail?" Bernard asked her.

"Oh, yes, yes," she said. "Of course. Y'all was on the second floor, and y'all used to send us messages down to the first floor in those little cups."

"That's right," Bernard laughed. "We did, didn't we?"

Decades had passed, yet Bernard and his fellow Rider were quick to return to their shorthand, exchanging memories in a way that left those of us on the outside only half grasping the stories they told. What I had little trouble understanding, however, was the indelible mark the Freedom Rides left on the Riders; each detail was seemingly seared into their memories, unforgettable, even after all this time. They shared stories I had never heard before.

"You hear about the time we tried to brew beer out of white potatoes?" Bernard asked. "Or how about the time we made chess pieces out of our bread?" With each new glimpse my heart soared higher. These, after all, were the moments that mattered to me most—the ones that had never quite found their way into the history books. "Well you've surely heard the story about the radio," Bernard said to his fellow Freedom Rider.

"You know," she pondered, "I don't think I have."

"Really?" he asked. "Well, it's a good one."

Taking our cue, the other eavesdroppers and I leaned in close for a listen. As if noticing us for the first time, Bernard turned our way, then regaled us with stories of the Nashville Quartet, a makeshift singing group that passed its time in jail by singing freedom songs. Initially the quartet consisted of Bernard and three of his fellow students from American Baptist Theological—James Bevel, Joseph Carter, and Samuel Collier—but since Sam wasn't arrested with the other Riders, their quartet was transformed to a trio.

"So we started singing one night," Bernard recalled, "and once we finished, the jailer comes by and says, 'Give me your radio.' Now, Bevel was always a clown," he noted, "so he told the jailer, 'We ain't gonna give you our radio.' Next thing we know we've got ten deputies around the cell. They were gonna beat us up until they got that radio."

Our smiles matched Bernard's own boyish grin as he continued his story with gusto. "I said, 'Look, Bevel, there's no sense getting beaten up over this.' And finally he says, 'All right, we'll give you the radio.' So we started singing again. I was just hoping we sang as good the second time as we did the first time.

And apparently we did," Bernard concluded, "because they were stunned."

I marveled at the tale—it confirmed a resilience that was all but impossible for me to understand. How, in the midst of such discord, were the Riders still able to create harmonious music together? How did they manage to find a bit of humor amid the heartache, all while playing a pretty good prank on their jailers?

Just as I began to think no story could top that one, Bernard started in on the next. "You know, Hinds [County Jail] wasn't really so bad," he recalled, running his fingers through his salt-and-pepper beard. "At least we got ice cream every night."

Collectively our eyes widened. From a few feet behind, I asked the obvious question: "So how'd you get ice cream?"

"Well, you see, the night warden was always sitting up there with us," Bernard explained, "and he'd be watching this old black-and-white television. Now what happened was, he liked our songs. He used to listen when we'd sing. I could see his reflection in a glass window, so I'd see him sneaking up to our cell against the wall. He'd get closer and closer, just listening, and we'd be serenading him. Sometimes we'd even put his name in the songs." Bernard laughed. "We called him 'professor' since we were all students."

Soon after their singing began, the night warden started rewarding Bernard and his cellmates with cardboard pints of ice cream, which he would hide in a mop bucket. Once the contraband was assembled, he would have a trustee place a dry mop atop the ice cream pints, then wheel the bucket toward their cell. "The trustee would roll it past all the other cells till he got to our cell," Bernard continued. "Then he'd lift the mop off, and we'd stick our hands through the bars. Once we were finished eating, we'd put our cardboard empties right back in that bucket. None of the others ever knew."

Bernard explained that their songs served as some much-needed common ground between the Riders and the night warden; their music managed to humanize the people on both sides of the bars. For the night warden the Riders were suddenly more than mere rabble-rousers. And as Bernard soon learned, the warden himself was more than just another white man wielding a billy club. He was a father, too, and his daughter was a junior in high school who had her heart set on attending college. "No one in his family had ever gone to college," Bernard said. "So we started telling him what she'd need to do. How to send out the applications and financial aid and all that. What better way to learn how to go to college," he asked, "than by talking to a cell full of college students?"

I smiled at the image of a clean-cut, mustachioed twenty-year-old Bernard detailing this information to the warden, as well as at the equally wondrous image of the white, middle-aged warden jotting down notes. In an unexpected turn of events, their roles had momentarily reversed: the student had become the professor, and the professor had become the student.

"Anyway, we got to be real good friends," Bernard concluded. "When they were shifting us out, he shook all of our hands and said it was one of the best experiences he'd had."

As Bernard's story wound down, the crowd thanked him and shuffled on. That was when I step forward to introduce myself. "B. J. Hollars," I said, extending my hand, "the guy who keeps bugging you with phone calls."

"There he is." Bernard smiled. "See? What'd I tell you? I knew we'd find time to talk."

That made one of us. Even though I knew Bernard had every intention of chatting with me, I also knew how easy it was for plans to go awry. As the Freedom Riders know better than most, it doesn't take much for one's route to become disrupted.

"So what's it like being back in this place?" I asked. "Especially on the anniversary of the beating?"

Bernard slipped his hands into his pockets as his eyes scanned the room. "Well, I've been back a number of times," he said at last. "But I'll be honest with you. When I was the dean of the graduate school right up the road at Alabama State, I never once came down here. Not once. There was kind of an emotional disconnect, I think."

"Does it take fifty-five years for that kind of emotional wound to heal?" I asked.

"Oh," he answered, his eyes drifting back toward the mug shots, "that wound never fully heals."

He was hardly the first Freedom Rider to explain that the physical wounds always healed faster than the emotional ones. And Bernard should know. On May 20, 1961, he was the target of both. Riders like Jim Zwerg, John Lewis, and William Barbee endured the brunt of the beating at the hands of the mob, but others, like Bernard LaFayette, Allen Cason, and Freddie Leonard, faced a slightly better fate—they remained conscious, at least, although Bernard, like Zwerg, suffered a few cracked ribs.

"It happened right there," Bernard told me, nodding to the front of the former bus station. "They were going to push me over that banister there. And it was a deep drop. But instead of allowing them to push me, Allen,

Freddie, and I turned around and just jumped down ourselves." Bernard described how he and the others took refuge on a raised platform at the post office located directly behind the station. This was safer ground, Bernard assumed, given that the post office was on federal property—a designation that ensured that any crime committed on it would be charged as a federal crime. It's unclear whether the mob understood the intricacies of the law, but they did turn their attention to easier prey: Zwerg, Lewis, and Barbee, all of whom were well within arm's reach.

"We saw it all," Bernard said. "There was this rail next to where the buses came in, and I watched them pick up Jim Zwerg and knock him over that rail five times." Bernard paused uncharacteristically, his eyes glued to the museum's front door. "It wasn't until I explained this to Jim a couple years back that he even knew what they'd done," Bernard said, returning his gaze in my direction. "You know, it's a miracle he's even alive."

=====

Two years after the events at the Montgomery Greyhound station, Bernard found himself facing his own close call with death. In the early morning hours of June 12, 1963, he—along with Mississippi NAACP Field Secretary Medgar Evers and the activist preacher Reverend Ben Elton Cox— were targeted for assassination. All three men were known to organize and inspire, skills that probably drew the attention of the would-be assassins. Evers lost his life that night.

"It was a tristate conspiracy," Bernard informed me.

"I'm sorry—what?" I asked. In all my research, I had never heard so much as a whisper of any tristate assassination conspiracy. "This happened the same night Evers died?"

"Oh yeah," Bernard confirmed. "The FBI told me all about it later. They had me slated to be killed in Selma."

I did not need to ask who "they" were, but Bernard offered the information all the same: a pair of white men who had stationed themselves in a pink and white Chevy just outside Bernard's home. One man sat in the driver's seat while the other peered under the hood. After returning home from a mass meeting—much as Evers did two hundred miles to the west— Bernard parked his car in the driveway and walked toward his house. He made it only a few steps, however, before the sound of crackling leaves prompted him to turn. Emerging from the shadows just ahead of him stood a man with a crew cut and exposed biceps. "Buddy," the man called, "how much would you charge for a push?"

In his book, Bernard offered the details of what happened next. After considering the risks, he agreed to help the man, so he returned to his 1948 Chevy and aligned his bumper directly alongside the bumper of the allegedly stalled car. From his place in the driver's seat Bernard waited for the signal to push, growing ever more impatient as the white men continued whispering to each other instead. Bernard kept a close eye on the silhouetted figures, and finally one man headed his way.

Bernard asked if the bumpers were properly aligned, to which the man replied that it was probably best if Bernard had a look himself. "It seemed odd," Bernard recalled later, "but I got out and bent over to check the bumpers." He was immediately assaulted; the man bludgeoned him with the butt of his gun, and Bernard collapsed on the pavement. He pulled himself up, staggering as his blood-filled eyes stared down his attacker. This was precisely what he had learned in James Lawson's training all those years before: that the best way to combat one's attacker was to face him. Rather than fight back, however, Bernard began hollering for his upstairs neighbor, a man named Red.

"Even in the midst of this attack I knew it was important for someone to witness what was happening," Bernard later wrote. Yet Red—as fiery as his name—refused to merely serve as a witness. Instead he aimed his rifle directly at the attackers. "Don't shoot him, Red!" Bernard shouted. After a confused moment, the white men—perhaps fearing that Bernard's plea might go unheeded—abandoned their mission, their tires squealing into the night as they sped away.

"They were going to—kill you," I said dumbly.

"Well, eventually," Bernard agreed. "But first they were going to kidnap me, then do to me like they did to Emmett Till."

———

These days almost everyone knows what Roy Bryant and J. W. Milam did to Emmett Till. On a warm Mississippi night in August 1955 they murdered the fourteen-year-old boy from Chicago for allegedly whistling at Bryant's wife—a claim Carolyn Bryant recanted in 2017, 63 years too late. On that August night in 1955 Bryant and Milam kidnapped him, beat him mercilessly, shot him, tied a cotton gin to his neck, and dumped his body into the Tallahatchie River. Till was pulled from the river three days later, his body all but unrecognizable.

Bernard, born just a year before Till, might easily have shared that fate. So would any other black man from that era who was believed to have committed such an act. For segregationists, Bernard's offense was obvious: he was a young black man in America fighting for rights that were legally his. Worse still, like Dr. King he appeared undeterred by the many threats to his life.

"Now there's one thing you must write," Bernard instructed, cornering me next to the museum's wall of mug shots, "because I want this spread out as far as possible." I nodded, holding my pen tight. He delved into what has long been a debate within the Freedom Riders' world: Why didn't Dr. King board the bus along with the Riders? Although this may seem to be a minor question, given Dr. King's larger legacy, for many Freedom Riders (Bernard included) it's one that often requires addressing.

Upon the release of the 2014 film *Selma*, the question returned to the forefront once more. "I told the producer he overlooked a very important thing," Bernard said, "because the film kind of gives the impressions that Martin Luther King was afraid to go on the Freedom Rides. But if he was afraid, he wouldn't have been there in the first place."

At the urging of Diane Nash and others, on May 21—the night following the trouble at the Greyhound station—Dr. King did join the Riders at Reverend Ralph Abernathy's First Baptist Church. His presence, meant to be a show of public support, also served to further inflame the city's already angered white segregationists. "He came into the city on the knife's edge of tension," read an editorial in the *Birmingham News*, "and went through the heart of Montgomery in a motorcade which was described by one observer as 'just like the President coming to town.'"

That night Reverend Abernathy's church became a "Who's Who" of the civil rights movement, hosting (in addition to Dr. King) Reverend Shuttlesworth, SCLC Executive Director Wyatt Tee Walker, and CORE National Director James Farmer. There were an impressive number of well-known Freedom Riders and foot soldiers as well, including John Lewis, Diane Nash, and Bernard. Fifteen hundred or so supporters packed the pews alongside them while a mob nearly twice that size took its place on the periphery.

According to *Time* magazine, in the moments just before the rally, the Riders "clustered together and clasped hands like a football team about to take the field." Then Reverend Abernathy took to the microphone, and in his booming voice he announced, "Ladies and gentleman, the Freedom Riders!"

The heroes' welcome was short-lived, however. Since warrants were out for their arrest, many of the Riders quickly faded into the crowd; some of them donned choir robes and spread out inconspicuously throughout the sanctuary. As the rally wound down, it became clear to those inside the church that leaving was no longer an option. So the Freedom Riders and their supporters resigned themselves to their new role—prisoners in the pews—and peered out the stained-glass windows at a mob that showed no signs of leaving.

The Riders watched as cars were set aflame and as the marshals attempted to maintain law and order. However, what became increasingly evident to those trapped inside was that the marshals could hold back the mob for only so long. It made sense to call in the police, the state troopers, and the National Guard, but responding logically wasn't what Alabama governor John Patterson had in mind. In fact, the sheer lack of law enforcement was by design; it was Patterson's less than subtle attempt to leave those inside the church vulnerable.

As the siege dragged on with no end in sight, Dr. King took matters into his own hands. Retreating to the telephone in the church basement, he called Attorney General Robert Kennedy and began to negotiate directly. Dr. King encouraged Kennedy to send in additional marshals, to which Kennedy replied that reinforcements were already en route. Adding to this good news was that at around ten o'clock that night Governor Patterson grudgingly declared martial law. It was better to have the Alabama National Guard and the Montgomery police present, Patterson reasoned, than to be invaded by federal troops, as had been threatened. The evening was far from over, but it was a triumphant moment for those trapped inside the church. They won simply by not losing, by holding tight and waiting for help to arrive.

Just before sunrise, the National Guard began transporting the Freedom Riders to local houses—most notably, Dr. Richard Harris's house—signaling that the standoff had come to its end. In the newspaper reports that followed, the details mostly confirmed the scene I have described here. Yet the portion of the story I had never heard before—the version Bernard told—centered on Dr. King's role during that fateful evening while sequestered in the church.

In a 2011 piece for the *New York Times*, Bernard first elaborated on a little-known detail from the night the Riders were trapped inside the First Baptist Church. According to him, at some point that evening Dr. King peered out at the crowd and asked for volunteers to carry out a "special mission." The only qualification was that the volunteers commit themselves to nonviolence.

Many black Montgomerians in the crowd that night had a hard time submitting to this qualification. In fact, several in the church were already armed, and for many of them the prospect of a nonviolent "special mission"—even one called for by Dr. King—wasn't a popular option.

Nevertheless, a small group of volunteers eventually emerged, at which point Dr. King explained the details of the mission in full. He had received word, he explained, that some black cab drivers were in the process of arming themselves at a nearby gas station in preparation for a battle with the mob.

"Some of these men were war veterans," Bernard wrote; "some were experienced hunters and were probably more experienced with weapons than their white antagonists. Had these men attacked the mob surrounding the church, the story of the Freedom Rides would have had a much different ending."

From his place in the pews, twenty-year-old Bernard watched dumbfounded as this small, unarmed force marched out of the church past the howling mob and in the direction of the armed cab drivers. "I was sure," he recalled, "I would never see them again." Yet within an hour the volunteers returned unscathed, their mission a success. Not only had they deterred the cab drivers and maintained the peace, they had done so without receiving so much as a scratch.

Dr. King had taken a chance on peace, and the risk paid off. "And that's why King couldn't join the Freedom Rides," Bernard concluded. "It was more important to have him as a leader than have him locked behind bars."

Near the end of my time at the Freedom Rides Museum, I met a woman named Dr. Valda Montgomery. We shook hands, and after a few minutes of chitchat she mentioned that she was the daughter of Dr. Richard Harris and that she had been thirteen years old when her father opened their home to the Freedom Riders. In addition, she and her family were neighbors of the Kings, whose parsonage home was located just two houses down South Jackson Street. I was dumbfounded by our serendipitous meeting, and when at last I found my tongue I asked what it was like growing up in that house, surrounded by so much history in the making.

"Well, it was something all right," she replied. "Why don't you come over some time and see the place for yourself?" Two days later I took her up on it. Walking past the Kings' parsonage house, I spotted Valda waving to me from beneath the green-and-white-striped awning of her family home. "Good morning!" she called. "Welcome."

I met her on the porch, pausing for a moment to consider the civil rights icons, foot soldiers, and Freedom Riders who had stood here before me. This was the porch the Kings frequented when stopping by for a neighborly chat. And it's the porch where Bernard LaFayette and the other Riders once hustled inside after the mob-filled mayhem at the church. "So much has happened here," I said, thinking out loud.

"Oh, all kinds of things," Valda agreed, nodding toward the house. "In fact, I think John Lewis said my dad gave him his first beer here." I smiled at this latest tidbit of history—another detail that, though hardly worthy of space on the home's historical marker, helped me humanize the larger civil rights story in my head.

From our place on the porch, Valda gave me the rundown on her family. She was one of four children, she told me, and even though she and her siblings never asked to be part of the civil rights movement, growing up in their household all but assured them a role. Valda's own involvement began when she was eight years old, in the midst of the Montgomery Bus Boycott.

"By the time I was eight my innocence was gone," she said. "From that point on it was nothing but civil rights, civil rights, civil rights. Nothing but marches and marches and marches. There were always barriers and obstacles and George Wallaces standing in doorways. And then, of course, there were the killings: [President] Kennedy, Malcolm X, Medgar Evers. And when they killed King—well, that was like losing an uncle."

Their families were close, she explained, and even though the Harrises were Catholic and therefore not parishioners at Dexter Avenue Baptist Church, this difference in faith did not keep them from socializing with each other. When Dr. King and his wife, Coretta, moved into the parsonage house in 1954, seven-year-old Valda and her siblings regularly made themselves at home in the young couple's new residence. The kids had grown familiar with the house because of its former occupants—the Reverend Vernon Johns and his family—and when the Kings moved in, the Harris children simply continued their occasional romp through the house, just as they had always done. In particular, Valda remembered playing in Dr. King's wood-paneled study as well as hearing Coretta play the scales on her piano.

The Harris children's interactions with the Kings only increased upon the births of Yolanda and Martin III, both of whom Valda and her older sister loved to look after. Valda recalled that the young friends spent many an afternoon plucking figs from the backyard trees and wading in kiddie pools.

One story that stood out for me and further humanized Dr. King involved Valda's brother Ricky. Though just three at the time, the boy remained vigilant regarding the condition of the whitewall tires on Dr. King's Pontiac sedan. Ricky regularly gave Dr. King a hard time about the tires ("Dirty, dirty, dirty," the child cried), prompting Dr. King to report directly to Ricky every time he got his tires cleaned.

Thus, although Dr. King was soon destined for worldwide acclaim, between 1954 and 1960 he was "just a neighbor" to Valda and her family. "He'd always walk up and down the street," she explained. "He'd go shoot pool on that corner, go across the street to get his hair cut." I smiled at the intimacy of these details, realizing that the larger-than-life image of Dr. King was but one view; in another he was simply a guy who chalked his pool cue and sat in a barber chair just like anyone else.

Although the King family moved to Atlanta in 1960, Dr. King's relationship with Dr. Harris remained close. "Any time there was something going on in Montgomery," Valda recalled, "King would know to give my daddy a call." That was perhaps how the Freedom Riders found themselves inside the Harris home early in the morning on May 22. Yet even now Valda wasn't certain just how those details were worked out. Did Dr. King personally arrange for the Freedom Riders to stay at the Harris house, or had someone else made the call?

Decades after Bernard was a houseguest in Valda's home, the pair reconnected and discussed this very question. Bernard told her that he too was uncertain of the details surrounding the decision, but he speculated that perhaps the National Guard had agreed to escort the Riders to the Harris home because of Richard Harris's past service as a Tuskegee airman—the military connection provided a deeper level of trust. Perhaps, Valda agreed, but she didn't know for sure.

One way or another, however, the Freedom Riders had found their way to the Harris home that morning, stepping inside the very doorway that Valda was now leading me through. Together we walked past the staircase on the left and the sitting room on the right and made our way to the kitchen, near the back of the house. It was a chef's dream, complete with a commercial-size cooking range with a ventilation hood. Just beyond it was a set of green stools around a counter. My eyes scanned the wooden cabinets, the refrigerator, and an old Coca-Cola box. Most of these items had come directly from Dr. Harris's store, creating an in-house lunch-counter vibe. To the left and a few steps up was the living room, complete with bookshelves and a big television screen blaring *Jeopardy.*

I recognized these rooms from the photos snapped fifty-five years earlier, old black-and-white shots documenting the days in late May 1961 when the Freedom Riders called this place home. "When you look at those photos," Valda said, "you'll see a lot of the things are still here. You'll see the hood, the cabinets, the refrigerator. There's one photo of King standing right over there," she said, pointing to the right edge of the kitchen. "He's with [Joseph]

Lowery, Abernathy, A. D. King, and a fifth person. And there's another one right by this fridge," she continued, leading us a few steps to the right. "In it you'll see Diane Nash talking to King. Because of the height of the fridge, you'll see that King wasn't a very tall person."

She continued her tour by leading us toward the stools. "And here," she said, tapping one of them, "is where James Farmer sat during some of the planning sessions."

"Right here?" I asked. "This exact stool?"

"Sure," Valda said. "Before [the stools] were here they were in Daddy's pharmacy. You'd be surprised how many civil rights folks probably ate at these stools: Rosa Parks, Fred Gray, the Freedom Riders . . . "

Valda recalled wandering down the stairs on the morning of May 22 to find a bedraggled crew of young men and women freshly escorted to her home from the previous night's siege at the church. She wondered where all the people had come from, but she didn't have a chance to find out before being shuffled off to school. It wasn't until later that afternoon that her question was answered, and even then the gravity of the situation failed to sink in. After all, it was hardly unusual for the Harris house to be bustling with people, and Valda figured that her father had simply invited a few friends over. "Now that I'm older," she added, "I'm wondering, 'Well, what did the neighbors think?' Surely they saw all of this activity going on."

If they had, they seemed to understand the level of secrecy required to ensure the safety of all involved. However, if the Harris family's harboring of Freedom Riders was a secret, Valda explained, then it was the worst-kept secret. She recalled one instance in which her loose-lipped younger brother wandered to a nearby white-owned grocery store to inform the clerk that he needed to buy some food for "all the visitors" living in their house. If the clerk caught on, he didn't mention it, and instead he simply rang up the sale.

"What do you remember about those nights with the Riders?" I asked, my hand lingering on a lunch-counter stool.

"I was thirteen," she reminded me, "so I'm remembering as a thirteen-year-old. And it was just a—just a party. People were just hanging out, and I'd sit and listen to them talk and laugh." Specifically, she remembered her uncle donating heaping plates of spaghetti from his restaurant to the hungry Riders, a surefire way to gather everyone in the kitchen. She also remembered continual card games played in all corners of the house, as well as the intensity with which the Riders would watch the news, wondering endlessly what would happen next.

Away at school for most of this, Valda wasn't privy to the minute-by-minute details of the day. But in the evenings she would poke her head into the strategy meetings and watch as Dr. King and the others struggled to hash out the details of what was to happen next.

When I asked Bernard about the nights he spent at the Harris house, he too spoke of the strategy sessions, describing one particularly contentious meeting for which he had the unenviable duty of serving as the chairman. At stake was whether to continue the Freedom Rides, and the opinions in the room were split. Yet the loudest voices belonged to those not present that night: Jim Zwerg and William Barbee, whose injuries were so extensive that they remained hospitalized just a few miles away at St. Jude's.

"There were warrants out for our arrest," Bernard reminded me, "[and] I was the designated guy to see how they were doing." After speaking with them, it was clear to Bernard that both men were in complete agreement that the Rides must continue, with or without them. Bernard took their message back to the Harris house later that night. "For me there was no question about whether we were going to continue the Ride," Bernard explained. "If those guys almost got killed and were ready to continue, I was convinced the rest of us should, too." Bernard's argument ultimately proved persuasive, and as a result the Ride rolled on.

Although key decisions such as this were made directly beneath her roof, at the time, thirteen-year-old Valda had little sense of her role as a witness to history.

"When did you start to understand the magnitude of what you experienced?" I asked.

"Not until I was grown," she said. "Not until right now."

=====

Back at the Freedom Rides Museum, the day at last wound down. By four o'clock in the afternoon most of the public was gone, leaving behind a dozen or so Freedom Riders to swap stories a while longer. From a few feet away I watched as they peered at the photos on the wall to identify their friends.

"Now that's John, isn't it?" one Freedom Rider asked.

"Sure is," another replied, "and that's Dennis right here."

Eventually Bernard wandered over to his friend and fellow Freedom Rider Rip Patton, and within moments they transported all of us back to the summer of 1961. I listened as Bernard steered the conversation back to where we had started earlier in the afternoon: with the story of the Nashville Quartet. Only this time he was speaking to an audience that already knew the story well. "Now back when we were in jail," Bernard said, "we had three-fourths of our quartet: me, Joe Carter, Bevel—"

"And then you found me," Rip added proudly, his voice a few octaves lower than Bernard's.

"You were the bass," Bernard noted. "We substituted you in for Sam."

"Substitute?" Rip shouted, feigning astonishment. "I'm just *now* finding out that I was a substitute! Fifty-five years later and you tell me this now."

"Well we needed your bass." Bernard laughed. The laughter drew everyone's attention, and a small crowd gathered. It was mostly Freedom Riders, but there were a few others as well: Dorothy Walker, the volunteers, and me, my notebook in hand.

And then suddenly, from out of that laughter, something magical happened: the Freedom Riders broke into song. They were no longer a quartet but had become a choir. Bernard's voice came in first, followed by Rip's, then Charles's, and then all the rest. "Woke up this morning with my mind stayed on freedom," they crooned. "I said I woke up this morning with my mind stayed on freedom. Well, I woke up this morning with my mind stayed on freedom. Hallelu, hallelu, hallelu."

Those of us on the periphery were floored. We looked at one another. *Is this really happening?* we wondered. All we knew for sure was that we were witnessing something spectacular: Freedom Riders singing in the very locale where, fifty-five years ago, several of them had been beaten. And because this moment would soon fade into history as well, the rest of us tried to take part in it. The volunteers and I began to clap, hum, and sing along as best we could. We wanted to feel the surge of power that they once felt, to know that transcendence firsthand.

For a brief moment, I almost thought I felt it: an unexplainable warmth washing over me as my own voice joined theirs. I knew only a few of the words, but that's all I needed to know. "Hallelu, hallelu, hallelu." By the song's end, everyone was laughing and giving each other bear hugs. There were promises to stay in touch, to see one another again real soon. "Let's not wait another five years," someone called out.

"Or another fifty-five!" shouted somebody else.

Bernard shook Rip's hand and told him he was a great addition to the quartet. "A substitute," Rip said in mock outrage. "You break it to me today."

I watched, a bystander, as the Freedom Riders made their way toward the door of that former bus station. Together they shuffled down the steps, descending into the hot Montgomery sun.

Figure 7. William "Bill" Harbour, mug shot, May 28, 1961.

Mississippi State Sovereignty Commission, "Mississippi State Sovereignty Commission Photograph," May 28, 1961, SCRID# 2-55-3-66-1-1-1ph, Series 2515: Mississippi State Sovereignty Commission Records, 1994–2006, Mississippi Department of Archives and History, February 20, 2017, http://mdah.ms.gov/arrec/digital_archives/sovcom/photo.php?display=item&oid=106.

6

Bill Harbour

Piedmont, Alabama

"It just happened so fast. And nobody understands that, how fast it all was. That mob came from just about every corner."

The Freedom Riders' song had barely dissipated before we reconvened, this time at Montgomery's First Baptist Church, just a mile from the former Greyhound station. It was the eve of the fifty-fifth anniversary of the church siege, and to commemorate the moment the Freedom Rides Museum had organized a community program complete with speakers, songs, and the guests of honor: a few dozen Freedom Riders, some of whom were returning to this place for the first time since that fateful night. This time, however, there would be no howling mob and no National Guard—just folks like me anxious to hear their stories.

When I entered the church, I was the only one there. The program wasn't scheduled to begin for another half hour or so, which gave me plenty of time to take it all in. From the back of the sanctuary I saw three sections of pews divided by aisles of red carpet. There was a piano, an organ, and, all around me, the room's beveled walls. Just behind me I felt a slight breeze, and I turned to notice the side door left slightly ajar—something that would never have happened fifty-five years earlier, when tear gas streamed down the street.

In my mind's eye I tried to conjure that terrible night—the flames, the fear, the people trapped in the pews—but it was hard, given the surrounding peacefulness. I peered up at the pulpit where Reverend Abernathy had preached week after week from 1952 to 1961—the same place from which Dr. King spoke, too, on the night the mob closed in. I shut my eyes, gripped the pew, and was transported back to that dark night in Montgomery when bricks were thrown, threats were hurled, and fifteen hundred human beings were just a firebomb away from their deaths.

How, I wondered, as I opened my eyes, could all that have happened here?

=====

It's hard to reconcile a place's past with its present. Bill Harbour knew this dichotomy all too well, given his own complex feelings toward the place he once called home. Born in the small town of Piedmont, Alabama, in 1942, Bill, the son of a cotton factory supervisor and the grandson of a sharecropper, spent much of his childhood performing the duties of the eldest son: plowing and picking cotton in his family's fields, often at the expense of his education. Yet with each acre plowed and each boll plucked, Bill began to realize just how much he hoped to pursue opportunities elsewhere, to leave behind his family and the fields and earn a college degree. This was no small undertaking, particularly for a nineteen-year-old black man in 1960. After his high school graduation (a class of 10), he applied to Jacksonville State University in nearby Anniston, a campus he'd grown familiar with from years spent chauffeuring his mother to and from work at the university's kitchen. Although it was an all-white campus, this hardly stopped Bill from applying.

However, word of this soon reached his father, Ade Harbour, along with a less than subtle message about his son's "mistake." That evening Harbour returned home livid. "Boy," he cried. "What are you messing with these white folks for?"

Of course, that hadn't been Bill's intention. He merely wanted an education at a university he had come to love—but as was now made clear, it hardly loved him back. Bill was crushed, not only by the university's rejection but also by his father's response. For the next several years Bill would face this particular conflict, pitting family against freedom, again and again.

With few prospects ahead of him, Bill left Piedmont for Nashville, hopeful that the larger city might offer new opportunities. One afternoon, after getting off at the wrong bus stop, he made the most of his error by taking a stroll along the quad at Tennessee Agricultural and Industrial State University, a historically black university. *Hey, this is a beautiful school*, he thought. He applied and was admitted soon after.

In the fall of 1960 Bill crossed paths with the future congressman John Lewis, who at the time was a twenty-year-old seminary student from another small Alabama town. Lewis took the Piedmont native under his wing, introducing him to others in the movement and helping him to get around Nashville. Indeed, the transition from small town to big city took some getting used to. (As Bill soon learned, his university's student body was nearly as large as the population of his hometown.) His time in Nashville also opened his eyes to the racial inequalities that had seemed less apparent to him while growing up in Piedmont.

"I guess blacks realized that they had their own place, and nobody tried to rock the boat," he reflected years later. "But when I got to Nashville I saw a chance to get in the movement and make a change."

Lewis soon acquainted Bill with several future Freedom Riders: Jim Zwerg, Bernard LaFayette Jr., and Catherine Burks, among others. In the months preceding the Ride, Bill joined the Nashville Student Movement's protest of the city's segregated movie theaters, a battle that proved particularly dangerous for Bill and Jim, both of whom were beaten as a result of their efforts to gain entrance. Yet as both men confirmed, these violent outbursts only served to embolden them, to remind them of the importance of their activism.

Just days after the successful integration of Nashville's theaters, Bill and Jim set their sights on the battle that lay ahead as they boarded a bus bound for Montgomery with the other newly recruited Freedom Riders. They weren't the first group of Freedom Riders, but the second: reinforcements committed to continuing the journey despite the Mother's Day violence in Anniston and Birmingham. The Nashville students had watched as the first wave of CORE-sponsored Riders (including Charles Person) barely escaped with their lives. Yet rather than allow the mob to declare victory by halting the Freedom Rides, the two young men boarded the buses themselves.

They too were beaten for it. Jim, as we know, endured injuries so severe that he was confined to a hospital bed for several days, which precluded him from joining his fellow Riders at the rally at the First Baptist Church on the evening of May 21. Bill's injuries were minor by comparison, allowing him to enter the church to a hero's welcome the night after the beating.

Tonight, fifty-five years later, he was present again—forced once more to reconcile his past with his present.

———

After half an hour or so of introductions, remarks, and thanks, we at last reached the portion of the program we had been waiting for: the Freedom

Riders recounting their tales. One after another they took to the mic to tell their piece of the story. It was a roll call I wished would never end, a sentiment seemingly shared by my wide-eyed seatmates in the pews.

"Any cause worth living for is a cause worth dying for," one Rider remarked, and another added, "Our job now is to pass the torch." Each Rider returned to the pews amid a series of "Amens," a confirmation of their truth. I myself adopted the bobble-head approach, nodding incessantly at every word spoken. I continued nodding as seventy-four-year-old Bill Harbour, the man I was here to see, casually strolled toward the podium, his red tie blazing beneath his suit coat. "My name is Bill Harbour," he began, as he headed toward the front of the room. "And—"

"Wait until you get to the mic!" hollered seventy-six-year-old Freedom Rider Catherine Burks-Brooks. The crowd chuckled at her chastisement, prompting Bill to shoot his old friend a look. "All right, then," he said, adjusting the mic and speaking directly into it. "Is this better?"

"Better," Catherine agreed.

"All right," he said again, clearing his throat. "Well, I was on the bus with Catherine Burks-Brooks there," he said, nodding to her, "and one night after getting arrested we got put out on a railroad track."

I leaned forward, eager for the story I knew was coming. It's one that has become the stuff of legends. Though just a footnote to America's larger civil rights story, it's a footnote worthy of a feature film.

After the arrest of several Freedom Riders in Birmingham on May 17, Bill explained, John Lewis, Catherine Burks, Lucretia Collins, and others were roused from their jail cells shortly after midnight and hustled into a pair of waiting limousines. Sitting in the front seat of the lead car was Bull Connor, Birmingham's commissioner of public safety and the rabid segregationist who, within another two years, had made his mark by ordering high-powered fire hoses aimed at peacefully protesting children.

Nineteen-year-old Bill took one look at the steely-eyed Connor and made his way toward the back of the car, whereas twenty-one-year-old Catherine, with fewer seats to choose from, soon found herself sandwiched between Connor and a police deputy in the front seat. Catherine later filled me in on every last detail of their midnight drive: the conversation, the emotions, the uncertainty. But when Bill told it from his place behind the podium, he opted for an abbreviated version, his attempt to stay within his allotted five minutes. "Bull told us he was gonna drive us back to Nashville," Bill explained, "and we believed him."

Instead, Connor escorted them to the Alabama-Tennessee border, dumped them along a dark stretch of highway, and pointed them toward a building he claimed was a train depot. It wasn't; it was just a locked warehouse not far from the railroad tracks. As the two cars' rear lights faded into the night, Bill, John Lewis, Catherine Burks, Lucretia Collins, and the others tried to reason their way out of their predicament, but their options were limited. In an effort to do something, Bill and a few of the men set off on a reconnaissance mission, but after fifteen minutes or so of finding nothing but wilderness, they reconvened with the larger group and started off together down the tracks. "We walked down the railroad track and found a house with a light on in the back," Bill remembered. "John Lewis and I knocked on the door."

A black man cracked open the door, took one look at the ragtag troupe of young people, and immediately closed it. Bill and the others managed to mention that they were Freedom Riders in need of help, but the claim seemed only to hasten the man's desire to lock the door. After all, it was a risk to even be seen with a Freedom Rider, let alone be seen assisting several under cover of darkness. "Now Catherine always got me in trouble," Bill joked, directing his eyes toward his friend. "You said to us, 'You didn't knock on that door loud enough to wake up his wife. Y'all know who's the boss of this house.' So we did," Bill said with a smirk, "and the wife said, 'Y'all children come on in.'" My eyes flitted to Catherine, seated a few rows up, and she confirmed the story with her smile.

Upon entering the strangers' home, the hungry and exhausted Riders took refuge as best they could. The woman sent her husband to buy food, which he did by stopping at various stores so as not to draw attention to his larger than normal food purchases. At some point during those early morning hours, a call was placed to Diane Nash in Nashville, who immediately dispatched civil rights activist Leo Lillard to rescue the stranded Riders. Disguising himself as a farmer, Leo borrowed Susan Wilbur's mother's car, then took to the Tennessee highway as the sun rose just beyond the horizon.

Although no one, including Lillard, could quite explain to me how he managed to find a random shack in Ardmore, Alabama, in the pre-GPS era, somehow he did (Ardmore was likely chosen for no particular reason other than it was near the Alabama-Tennessee state line). And by midmorning the Riders were squeezed tight into the car as they reversed the route they had taken the previous night. "We stayed in Birmingham for a couple of days before we left for Montgomery," Bill said, momentarily allowing his mind to drift. "It was tough in Montgomery. Here, it was tough."

He did not have to specify. By that point in the evening, even those in the pews who knew little of the Freedom Rides knew of the horrors that occurred at the Greyhound station. They knew about the beatings of Jim Zwerg, John Lewis, and William Barbee. And they knew about those who were mostly spared: Bill, Bernard LaFayette Jr., and Catherine Burks, among others. "But this church was here for us," Bill explained, peering out at the crowd. "It was nearly full of citizens from Montgomery. I don't know if they came to see what the Freedom Riders looked like, or what fools we were coming into Montgomery to get beat up."

Bill paused, resting his hands on the podium. "Every time I come into this church I think about how we used to sit there, and how they were turning cars over and setting them on fire right outside. It was a dark night, and we were here a long time." It was so long, in fact, that people in the pews began to nod off, even as the flames from the burning cars leapt high toward the stained-glass windows. "That was tough," Bill repeated, his eyes turning toward those windows. "That was *real* tough."

———

Back at the Freedom Rides Museum the following day, the reunion was coming to a close. Just ahead of me stood Bill Harbour, a man in high demand. From my place a few steps away, I watched as he signed books, posed for photos, and took a moment for every person who wanted to talk to him—including me. Even though he was running late, after I introduced myself he insisted that we sit down for a chat. We had been playing phone tag for weeks, and now that we were finally in the same room, we both wanted to make the most of it.

Bill excused himself from his crowd, then led me toward a white fold-up table on the opposite side of the museum, the former site of the "colored" waiting room. We pulled up chairs and got comfortable. "So tell me about that drive from Birmingham to Montgomery," I began. "I've heard it from Jim Zwerg and Bernard LaFayette, but how do *you* remember it?"

Much like Jim and Bernard, Bill too recalled the helicopters, the police escort, and the eerie quiet that befell the bus as their protection went away. "I remember pulling into *this* bus station," Bill recalled, tapping the table with his finger, "and John Lewis saying, 'It's mighty quiet here.'" I nodded. "It just happened so fast. And nobody understands that, how fast it all was. That mob came from just about every corner," he added, nodding at a few alleys across the street.

He described witnessing Bernard LaFayette Jr. and the others leaping over the rail toward the post office while he himself ran toward a taxi. "I saw a car. I didn't even know who was driving it. A black man [was]. So I said, 'Take me to a black neighborhood.' And he did. I didn't know what happened to the rest of them." That night, as they reconvened in the basement of First Baptist Church, the stories began to emerge: how some of the Riders had escaped, while others—Jim Zwerg, John Lewis, and William Barbee, in particular—were hardly so lucky.

Bill told me the same story he'd been telling for years: a version that had become his definitive account over time. It's so definitive that as I listened to him recite the details of that day, I noticed him repeating exact snippets I'd read in previous interviews he had given. After more than half a century of telling his tale, he had become a seasoned storyteller. But I wanted to hear the parts he had never told before; I wanted him to go off script. After a bit of coaxing, Bill began to open up, his eyes drifting toward the front of the Greyhound station as the poignancy of this place took hold of him. "What was going through your mind that day?" I asked. "What were you thinking?"

"Well, sometimes I still think about that bus," he confided, "and I wonder if the driver took out the keys [from the ignition]." Bill explained that he had driven a school bus for two years in high school, and in that time he had become quite adept behind the wheel. "You see, if the driver had left those keys in the ignition," he continued, "and if I saw that mob coming at us with those ax handles and everything—well, I wonder if maybe I'd have taken off. Just driven that bus on out of here."

It was part of the story I'd never heard before, straight from the mind of Bill Harbour. And even though it was merely hypothetical, I couldn't help but imagine an alternative version of history in which the front page of the *Montgomery Advertiser* depicted not a bleeding Jim Zwerg but instead a white-knuckled Bill Harbour steering them clear of danger.

"Excuse me," a woman cut in, "I hate to interrupt, but are you Bill Harbour?"

"I am," he acknowledged, smiling at the middle-aged woman before him.

"Would you mind signing a few of these books?"

He was happy to, and he flipped open one book after another and signed his name alongside his photo. But he could hardly flip a single page without pausing to point out his friends' photos. He introduced us to them one after another—Catherine Burks, Charles Person, Bernard LaFayette Jr.— then squinted as he searched for himself in a group photo. "Now where am

I in here?" he muttered, peering at a photo of the Riders in a waiting room. "I should be sitting next to John and Lucretia here." He was baffled by the lack of his presence, as if history had somehow rewritten itself without him. "Oh, *there* I am," he said with relief, pointing to himself in the photo. "Okay now. That's better."

His commentary continued for a few minutes, and the woman stood politely while Bill time-warped us to that era, recounting details about the people in all the photos. As he scrawled his name alongside his own photo, the woman said, "Well, I'm sure glad you lived to tell us this."

"*You're* glad?" he exclaimed, his face blossoming into a smile. "Yeah, me too."

———

In May 1961 Bill and many other college-age Freedom Riders were faced with a dilemma: Do we study history or do we make it? For many, the early Freedom Rides directly conflicted with final exams, placing student activists in a difficult spot. After all, missing an exam all but ensured a failing grade for the course, but as Bill knew all too well, the stakes were much higher than the classroom. Still, there were reputations to consider, especially when one hailed from Piedmont, Alabama.

"This all happened during my first year at Tennessee State," Bill told me. "And being from a small town, I couldn't afford to flunk out of school. People would talk about it. That was one of the major things on my mind: how I couldn't flunk out." Bill held the distinction of being the first person from Piedmont to ever attend Tennessee A&I, and he certainly didn't want to be the first to return home without a degree.

In the days after the trouble at the Montgomery bus station, Bill and fellow Tennessee A&I student Catherine Burks returned briefly to Nashville to take their final exams. Although Bill never wavered in his support of the movement, he also knew the importance of completing his education. To not complete it would have tarnished his reputation in Piedmont and potentially jeopardized his future. Then again, what good was a future without equality? And what good was a degree if skin color disqualified him from achieving his goals?

When I asked Bill what the Ride's darkest moment was, he informed me that it actually occurred after the Freedom Rides had concluded. "The only moment that bothered me was when we got out of jail and came back to school and were told we were gonna be expelled." Bill was shocked by the lack of support, particularly since the directive seemed to be coming from the university's black president, Dr. Walter Davis. It felt like a betrayal of the highest order, Bill explained, a confirmation that some black people in positions of power were refusing to acknowledge the Riders' sacrifice for the collective. "We were trying to help change society," Bill declared, dumbfounded, "so why would he expel us?"

Part of the answer probably lay in Dr. Davis's own predicament. As a black university president working under an all-white board, it's not hard to imagine the various influences at work. Nevertheless, Bill never forgave the betrayal. He had endured beatings at the hands of segregationists, but that was expected. What wasn't expected was an assault on his education, courtesy of a man he thought was an ally. "That was tough," he lamented, echoing the words he used the previous night in the church. "That was *real* tough."

But the betrayals didn't stop there.

Bill, like many of the Freedom Riders, served time at Parchman Farm, enduring one indignity after another as he counted the days to his release. In the waning days of his sentence, anguish emerged from an unexpected source. "I'd spent forty-nine days in prison," he told me, "and I was just getting ready to get out when my mother wrote me a painful letter."

Son, Catherine Harbour wrote, *I don't think you should come home. These folks are stirred up that you've been on the Freedom Ride. You better not come home right now.* For her it was a matter of safety, and even though she would miss her son terribly during his three years of exile, she also knew that the distance was the only way to ensure his well-being. "That made me feel real bad," Bill said, pausing to reveal a glimpse of emotion. "And I realized how painful it was for her to do that."

In a previous interview, I'd heard Bill explain how after his arrest in Birmingham, his father became a target, too. White men began intimidating Ade Harbour at the cotton factory where he worked, informing him that his son was "really messin' up." Later their intimidation reached the Harbour home as well; their phone rang throughout the night with threatening messages, a problem that could be solved only by removing the phone entirely.

Despite Ade Harbour's initial tongue-lashing in the aftermath of Bill's application to Jacksonville State University, neither he nor Catherine ever tried to steer their eldest son away from his civil rights work again. They were scared for him as well as for themselves, but they understood the importance of the fight. And if Bill was willing to put himself on the front lines, then they were willing to support him on the home front.

In June 1961 Bill's time on the front lines landed him in Parchman Farm, where he shared a cell with fellow Freedom Rider John Lewis, a man whose civil rights résumé was only just beginning. In his memoir *Walking with the Wind*, Lewis described Bill as being "small, even smaller than I, and very open, very talkative." He remembered, too, the way Bill and Bill's sister Liz had looked up to movement leaders—Diane Nash, Bernard LaFayette, James Bevel, and himself—"almost with awe. . . . If John Lewis said go," Lewis wrote, "Bill Harbour was ready to go." Bill concurred with this assessment.

"So what was it like being cellmates with John Lewis?" I ask. "What did you two do for so long in such close quarters?"

"Well," he answered, "you get pissed off, you hug, you raise hell— though I couldn't say that word too much because John was studying to be a minister at the theological seminary. So," Bill laughed, "I couldn't cuss too damn loud."

In many ways their prison experience was representative of that of many other Freedom Riders. Since cerebral opportunities were limited (no books, little or no paper), the prisoners often turned to prayer. Bill recalled an instance in which John tried to reassure him that God was going to take care of them and release them from their prison.

"He went on to talk about Shadrach, Meshach, and Abednego," Bill chuckled, referring to the Book of Daniel in the Bible, "and how God opened the jail and let them out and all this stuff. One time he even read a paragraph about how the jail doors flew open and they walked out. So I said, 'Wait a minute, John. If you believe that, then why aren't *our* doors flying open so we can get the hell out of here?'" Bill deeply admired his cellmate's faith and even shared it, but he was nevertheless reluctant to rely on God to unlock their prison door. Eventually the door would be flung open, not because of divine intervention but because of the Riders' willingness to wait.

Four days later, at Bill's behest, I drove to Jacksonville, Alabama, to meet Pete Conroy, the director of the Environmental Policy and Information Center at Jacksonville State University. He was also the cochairman with Bill for the development of Freedom Riders Park on the site of the Anniston bus firebombing. "Tell him I said hi," Bill had said. "Pete will tell you everything you need to know about the park."

Actually, until a few weeks ago, I hadn't even known there was a park in process. But thanks to the efforts of Bill Harbour, Charles Person, Pete Conroy, and a few state legislators and city councilmen, the push to establish Freedom Riders Park was coming closer to reality.

"Pete?" I called, poking my head into the dark entryway to his office.

The energetic fifty-eight-year-old glanced up from his magazine with a wide smile on his face. "You must be B. J.," he said, inviting me to sit down. The photographs lining his office walls made it clear to me that Pete was a man who got things done. My eyes flashed first to a photo of Pete posing alongside the Bushes, then another of him smiling alongside the Clintons. I was impressed by his access to leaders of the free world, but Pete brushed off my wide-eyed wonder, explaining that the photos were simply the result of having accepted environmental appointments in both administrations. He had also served five Alabama governors, utilizing his environmental policy expertise to establish thousands of acres of natural preserves and refuges throughout Alabama. For the moment, however, Pete was most excited to talk about his current project, the formation of Freedom Riders Park.

"It started around 2004," he explained, "when a progressive state Democrat approached me and said, 'Well, we're finally able to bulldoze that damn gas station.' I asked, 'What gas station?' And he said, 'Oh, you know, the one involved in that whole mess with the burning bus and the Freedom Riders.'" Pete said his jaw dropped. "That happened *here*?" he asked the man. Pete had lived in Anniston for nearly twenty years, yet in all that time he had never heard a whisper about the city's connection to the Freedom Riders.

When Pete heard of the plans to demolish the gas station, he wondered why they didn't preserve it instead. After all, it was part of history, he reasoned, even if many people would just as soon forget about it. By the time Pete got involved, however, the wrecking ball had already done its work, leaving no trace of the structure beyond the land itself. So Pete began working to acquire the land, and he eventually persuaded the state to transfer five acres to the county. State Representative Barbara Boyd drew up a resolution in support of the park, and a committee was assembled. Pete was asked to chair it, although he balked at the suggestion. It wasn't the work that bothered him, but the perception. "Frankly, as a white [man], I didn't feel comfortable serving as the sole chair for a project pertaining to civil rights," he told me. "I suggested Bill Harbour serve as cochair, and he agreed."

Plans were made, artistic renderings were commissioned, and in October 2012 a symbolic groundbreaking took place, complete with a thousand or so onlookers. A sign was unveiled introducing Anniston residents to the "Future Home of Freedom Riders Park"; it provided a detailed rendering of the proposed park, complete with a lush walkway of native plants leading toward a memorial sculpture. For Pete, Bill, and the park's many supporters, it was a moment of celebration. After years of work, their goal at last seemed within reach. Yet within weeks the sign was burned by vandals, a bone-chilling reminder that in Anniston the past is hardly past at all—even half a century later.

Despite this setback Bill and Pete continued to work hard to see the project through, bringing together all the right people, including Charles Person, who also served on the committee. "These guys are something," Pete told me. "When they started the Ride, Bill was nineteen. And Charles was only eighteen! For me it's mind-blowing. I was just a kid from Pennsylvania, maybe six or seven, when all of this was happening, so I didn't know anything. But I do kind of remember the images on an old black-and-white TV."

Because he had grown up in the all-white town of Lancaster, Pennsylvania, one of Pete's earliest memories of African Americans was the televised images of the burning bus. The images stayed with him all these years, and he was now committed to making sure that others remember as well. "It's a team effort," he told me, rising from his chair. "Now come on, it's time for lunch. And I want you to meet a part of the team."

———

Ten minutes later I parked my car alongside Pete's in a lot just off Anniston's main drag. It's just a few blocks from the town's Greyhound station, where fifty-five years ago the bus's tires were knifed by a mob, ensuring that the Freedom Riders would never make it to Birmingham. "You're going to like this place," Pete said as we entered the restaurant's back door. "They just remodeled it."

Pete directed us to a high-top table near the corner, where a man in a suit and tie awaited our arrival. "B. J., this is Seyram Selase," he said, introducing me to the thirty-two-year-old, "a city councilman here in Anniston. He's been a huge help with Freedom Riders Park. He represents the district where it'll be built."

"Welcome to Anniston," Seyram responded, smiling and shaking my hand. "How do you like it so far?"

"It's great," I said, "though admittedly I haven't seen very much of it."

Seyram, in contrast, had seen it all. Born and raised in Anniston, he spent his formative years in the city before enrolling at Berea College in Kentucky. "It wasn't until I got to Berea that I really became enamored with my African American history," he explained. "I actually minored in African American history, and once I began learning more, the impact of what happened right here in Anniston really began to blow my mind."

"When was the first time you heard of Anniston's role in the Freedom Rides?" I asked. "Did you learn about it in school?"

"Well, it was talked about in our elementary school," Seyram remembered, "but it's not like they ever took us on field trips to the site of the bus bombing. Granted, there wasn't really anything there to see, but they didn't even take us to the bus terminal." The irony, he described, was that the bus terminal was just a stone's throw away from his former school. Since he took office, however, things had changed. Today a commemorative bus mural adorns the alley adjacent to the station, and alongside it hang several placards dedicated to recounting the story.

"It's so great to watch these projects finally happen fifty-five years later," he told me. "I mean, the bus bombing was talked about a little, but in certain parts of the community it was still kind of hush-hush. People just wanted to move on. But for me, really understanding the importance of those events, that's what matters now. I work a lot in the schools," he added, "and I try to tell the story so the kids can know it happened right here."

"I love that our generation is now trying to tell the story, too," I said. "A lot of the Freedom Riders keep telling me that they feel like they dropped the torch, that they didn't tell their story enough. And I keep telling them, 'Let us help. You did the hard work, you boarded the bus. The least we can do is tell about what you did.'" Seyram agreed.

"What was it like growing up in Anniston?" I inquired.

"Well, there was not a lot of racism," he replied, "but there were some remnants of it that impacted me as a young African American [man]." He described an experience in which he and his friends were walking in the mall parking lot when a police car sped through the crosswalk, nearly plowing right over the entire group.

"We jumped back and was like, 'Hey man, what's going on?' and he shot us a bird and called 'Nigger!'"

"A cop did this?"

"Yeah. I was sixteen."

"And now," Pete said, nodding toward Seyram, "he's on the city council."

====

Later that afternoon I parked my car in front of Anniston's former Greyhound station. It appeared similar to the civil-rights-era pictures I had seen of it—a one-story brick building complete with a narrow alleyway, a design that assisted the mob by boxing the bus in on all sides. Today the alley serves as a stop on the Spirit of Anniston's Civil Rights Trail. As Seyram had described, alongside the life-size bus mural were placards, all of which provide background on the historical account of what happened on Mother's Day 1961.

By now I was well versed in the story, and what moved me most were the names of the Freedom Riders listed on the placard. I touched their names with my hand: Albert Bigelow, Ed Blankenheim, Genevieve Hughes, Jimmy McDonald, Mae Francis Moultrie, Joseph Perkins, and Hank Thomas. Today only Hank is still alive—the last living testament to a violent moment that nearly took all their lives. I had met him just days before at the Freedom Rides Museum in Montgomery; he was a hulking man with a voice so deep it rivaled that of Rip Patton, another Freedom Rider. Soon after the Anniston bus firebombing, Hank Thomas had rejoined the Ride, despite his near-death experience. It was a decision that sent a clear message to his perpetrators: the Freedom Riders would not be turned around, no matter what the price.

As with my experience at First Baptist Church, it was hard for me to comprehend the horror that once occurred here. Try as I might, I couldn't see the crowds descending, couldn't see the young white man lying prostrate in front of the bus's wheels to ensure it wouldn't move. The firsthand accounts of what happened that day in Anniston tell one version of the story, but Joe Postiglione's photos offer the most visceral version. Postiglione, a freelance photographer with the *Anniston Star*, happened to be on scene that fateful day, his camera fully loaded with film. After he had spent several hours shooting the dramatic scene, his visual proof of the encounter soon went public, gracing the front pages of newspapers and offering the nation another example of unspeakable violence at the hands of a mob. A week later the photograph of Jim Zwerg's blood-drenched body had a similar effect, serving as a vivid reminder to a national audience of the perils of vigilante action.

=====

Back behind the pulpit at First Baptist Church, Bill Harbour closed his remarks by reminding us that the world works in mysterious ways. He recounted his past desire to attend Jacksonville State University, informing those of us in the pews that every time he picked up his mother at work he would see the college and think to himself, "I'm going there one day." As we now know, it wasn't to be so. He had the right grades but the wrong skin color, and in that era the latter outweighed the former.

"They refused to let me go to Jacksonville State," Bill told us. "But guess what?" He paused for dramatic effect as we leaned forward, waiting for the good news we were so desperate to hear, some confirmation of a silver lining. "Four years ago," Bill said, tapping the podium, "I was the commencement speaker for Jacksonville State University." Right on cue, the crowd went wild. *I* went wild.

Bill knew a mic-drop moment when he heard one, so he took his leave at the height of the cheering, a firm smile fixed on his face. A smile broke across my own face as the applause echoed down from the rafters, much as it had fifty-five years ago, when Bill first took his place in that pew.

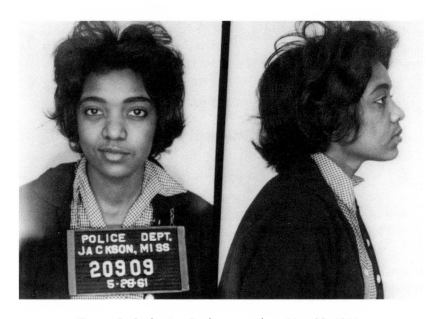

Figure 8. Catherine Burks, mug shot, May 28, 1961.

Mississippi State Sovereignty Commission, "Mississippi State Sovereignty Commission Photograph," May 28, 1961, SCRID# 2-55-3-71-1-1-1ph, Series 2515: Mississippi State Sovereignty Commission Records, 1994–2006, Mississippi Department of Archives and History, February 20, 2017, http://mdah.ms.gov/arrec/digital_archives/sovcom/photo.php?display=item&oid=110.

7

Catherine Burks

Birmingham, Alabama

"I could hear the white women screaming. And they had babies in their arms, but they kept screaming, 'Kill them niggers, kill them niggers.'"

At a few minutes past 7:30 A.M. on May 25, 2016, I took a seat on a bench in Birmingham's Kelly Ingram Park. It was my thirty-second birthday, and to celebrate I ate some cold oatmeal alone. The park was empty, but on its periphery I spotted a local news team as well as a cadre of hardly inconspicuous Federal Bureau of Investigation agents, a few of whom gave me the once-over to ensure that my eating-oatmeal-in-a-park proclivities didn't translate to me being a threat. They were on high alert, and for good reason. After all, it's not every day that the FBI director pays a visit to the 16th Street Baptist Church.

Kelly Ingram Park became famous (or perhaps notorious) for the Children's Crusade—demonstrations immortalized in the graphic photos of fire hoses turned toward young demonstrators—but it also shares a civil rights history with the church just across the street. There, inside the stone walls of the 16th Street Baptist Church, a bomb exploded, killing four girls on the morning of September 15, 1963. Their names (and ages) were Addie Mae Collins (14), Cynthia Wesley (14), Carole Robertson (14), and Carole Denise McNair (11). Their deaths spurred immediate outrage, even prompting some white southerners to rethink the methods used to maintain the status quo.

Charles Morgan Jr. (Chuck, to his friends) is the man most remembered for speaking his mind in the wake of the tragedy. A white Birmingham lawyer with a progressive streak, Chuck had watched his city unravel for years as a result of racial unease. Finally, on the day after the blast, Chuck made his feelings publicly known. The thirty-three-year-old offered a scathing rebuke of southern culture while speaking before the Birmingham Young Men's Business Club, of which he was a member.

"Four little girls were killed in Birmingham yesterday," he began. "A mad, remorseful worried community asks, 'Who did it? Who threw that bomb? Was it a Negro or a white?' The answer should be 'We all did it.' Every last one of us is condemned for that crime and the bombing before it and a decade ago. We all did it."

We all did it. With those four words he made the nation complicit in the girls' deaths. There was no more sitting it out on the sidelines, no more blind-eye approaches to the violent crimes wrought against blacks. Morgan believed it was high time for people to stand up and be counted—and announce whose side they were on.

Those in the crowd that day offered a smattering of polite applause, but Morgan's words spurred little action. Moments later, in fact, when a member suggested that a "Negro" might be invited to join the club, the idea was quickly shot down. It was one thing to agree with Chuck Morgan in theory but quite another to invite a "Negro" into their ranks.

As a result of his tongue-lashing, Morgan and his family soon became targets themselves. The threats were relentless (and in a few instances, credible), so within a few months the Morgan family packed up and left Birmingham altogether.

Sitting on that Birmingham bench fifty-three years later, I wondered: Would I have spoken out?

=====

Catherine Burks (now known as Catherine Burks-Brooks) had never had a problem speaking out. In fact, her sharp-tongued barbs had become her hallmark. She was a woman with a reputation for speaking the truth, even to those who wanted to hear it the least—a trait she shared with Chuck Morgan.

Born in Birmingham, Catherine was the youngest in a family of six—a birth order she credited for her fighting spirit. Despite being several years younger than her siblings, she always managed to hold her own, a skill she continued to hone throughout her most active years in the civil rights movement. However, her instinct to hold her own first developed when she faced opposition to becoming a majorette in her high school marching band. Parker High School was one of the largest black schools in the country at the time, yet even there Catherine faced discrimination—a result not of the color of her skin but of its shade; historically, the majorettes at Parker High had always been light-skinned. Catherine and two other dark-skinned students refused to be turned away, however. Eventually their band director relented, although from that point on, Catherine recalled, he always affectionately referred to them as his "three little darkies." It was an odd entrance into the world of activism, but it reaffirmed for Catherine the importance of fighting for justice—no matter who was the oppressor.

In 1960 Catherine enrolled in Tennessee A&I, joining Bill Harbour, Rip Patton, and several other future Freedom Riders—all of whom would later be expelled as a result of their civil rights involvement. Until her dismissal, Catherine enjoyed her time at the college, in particular the civil rights opportunities available to her and the relationships forged along the way. Both elements converged in the fall of 1960, when Catherine ramped up her civil rights efforts as a result of her boyfriend at the time, Curtis Murphy—who, she suspected, was eyeing the coeds from Fisk University who regularly attended the mass meetings.

Although Catherine's initial impetus to attend the mass meetings was partly motivated by her desire to keep an eye on Curtis, her commitment to the cause only grew, even as her relationship with Curtis fizzled. As fate would have it, she met her husband, Paul Brooks, while attending those meetings. They dated throughout their time on the Freedom Rides and married in August 1961, not long after Catherine's release from Parchman. Although they eventually separated, for decades Catherine and Paul shared their lives, committing much of their life together to the cause of civil rights. After the Freedom Rides, Catherine and Paul participated in voter registration drives in Mississippi, then went on to coedit the *Mississippi Free Press*, an alternative newspaper focused on civil rights.

Later Catherine held a number of other jobs as well, from teaching in both the Chicago and Nashville public schools to pursuing social work in Detroit. In Detroit she and her husband Paul opened a shop that specialized in African-inspired clothing and jewelry. During that time Paul received a design patent for a new version of the Afro pick, which did much to support the family financially. After several years in the Bahamas, Catherine returned to Birmingham, where she began working for Avon in 1979 and rose to become a district sales manager before retiring from the company in 1997. She then became a substitute teacher in Birmingham for the next several years. Despite all these experiences, nothing ever compared to her time on the Freedom Rides and, in particular, the night she spoke the truth to Bull Connor.

———

In the minutes before FBI Director James Comey took to the pulpit at the 16th Street Baptist Church, I slipped into a pew near the back. My mind was on Catherine, whom I was slated to visit later that afternoon. But my mind was also on the four girls whose martyrdom forever changed this church, this city, and the country at large. I wondered if any of them might have attended Parker High School, like Catherine, and aspired to be majorettes.

I admit I hadn't emotionally prepared myself for taking a seat in this church. Twenty-four hours earlier, in fact, I had had no intention of visiting at all. I didn't want to be viewed as another white northern "tragedy tourist"—someone who only stopped long enough to snap a photo, shake his head, and then abruptly forget. But upon learning of Director Comey's visit, I now had a reason to go, as well as the opportunity to spend some time remembering the tragedy that most people might just as soon forget.

The people in the pews around me were pastors, community members, and law enforcement officers, and the latter prominently displayed the badges around their necks and the guns holstered on their hips. I'd never seen a gun in a church before, and it was startling, despite the fact that the badges confirmed I had nothing to fear—that is, I, a white man, had nothing to fear. I wondered if the black people in the pews felt differently; for them, a badge and a gun offered a more muddled message. Certainly history, including recent history, allowed for a varied interpretation. It's a message that Director Comey himself acknowledged moments later, after taking to the pulpit amid our applause.

The clean-cut, six-foot-eight fifty-five-year-old hardly fit the image of an FBI director that I had concocted in my head—because that image was largely inspired by the bureau's first director, J. Edgar Hoover. Before this morning, all I knew about Comey was what I had learned from thirty-second sound bites, and although I had mostly liked what I'd heard, I'd still imagined him to be cut from the same cloth as Hoover. After all, it takes a certain kind of person to oversee the FBI, and in my mind that person was tight-lipped, dour-faced, and mostly hidden from public view.

Yet as he took his place before us, it was evident that Comey exhibited none of these characteristics. Within a few lines he proved himself to be a thoughtful, well-spoken man whose views on national security—as well as the scope of the FBI's reach—mostly aligned with my own. Public perceptions of Comey certainly became more complicated in the days leading up to the 2016 presidential election—and even more complicated than that after President Donald Trump fired Comey in May 2017—but before any of those headlines, as he stood behind that pulpit, he was still clear of controversy. He was also acutely aware of his surroundings—namely, what it meant to be a white man speaking within the sanctity of this church.

"When I was in college," Comey began, "I took a class called Significant Books in Western Religion. There were only twelve books studied during that semester, and one of them was actually not a book at all. It was a letter. It was Martin Luther King's 'Letter from Birmingham Jail.'" I nodded knowingly as Comey described King's letter as a "seminal work about justice and humanity" as well as "one of the most important things" he'd ever read. "Dr. King's message, as you know, is about achieving justice in an imperfect world," he continued. "It's about striving for equality in a world that is inherently unfair. It's about connections as people, as communities, and as a country."

For much of the speech Comey described the importance of these connections—confirming the FBI's commitment to strengthening them while also acknowledging that this goal could be achieved only by earning the community's trust. And, he was quick to admit, it was a trust that had been broken before. "Before the Civil Rights Act of 1964, " Comey continued, "the federal government left protection of civil rights to state and local governments. As you know all too well, many murders went uninvestigated or were covered up or were misidentified as an accident. Evidence was scarce, prosecution was really hard, and trails ran cold."

Yet as a result of the Civil Rights Act—as well as some of the FBI's more public missteps (the example he gave was when the bureau wiretapped Dr. King)—the bureau recommitted itself to protecting the civil rights of all Americans, regardless of skin color. "We were late to this fight. That is true," Comey admitted. As a result, he explained, the "disconnect between communities and law enforcement officers" still remained. And more often than not, he added, the communities facing the greatest disconnect were communities of color.

Throughout his speech Comey hit all the right notes, walking a fine line between mea culpas and throwing the bureau under the proverbial bus. His words, though conciliatory, were far from a condemnation aimed at law enforcement—a wise rhetorical choice, given the number of officers populating the pews.

He concluded his speech by shifting the focus forward. "I think if Dr. King were with us today, he would suggest to us ways to have these difficult conversations. He would urge the rest of the country, I suspect, to have the conversations the way they have them in Birmingham. I think he would tell us to work to have open hearts and open minds, and to see others more clearly. Because," he said, emphasizing each word as his speech reached its crescendo, "it is hard to hate up close."

A wave of murmurs drifted through the church, followed by more than a few "Amens."

"It is hard to hate someone you know," he reiterated, summoning his pastoral voice, "someone whose life you have come to understand." His words echoed a sentiment I had heard shared by several Freedom Riders: how crucial it is for those practicing nonviolence to make every effort to humanize themselves in the eyes of the oppressor. When one segment of the population continually dehumanizes another, it's easier to hurl a bomb into a church. And it's easier to aim a fire hose at black children, too, when the man wielding the hose views them as a problem rather than as people. Hate allowed for the unleashing of police dogs, the beatings of Riders, and the hanging of people from trees. Yet when oppressors come to know those they oppress—endowing people with names, families, and life stories—suddenly it's more difficult to carry out such heinous acts.

Restraint is as important as empathy. As Comey conceded, the FBI's past use of restraint didn't always live up to the bureau's high standards. To illustrate, he described a memo dated October 10, 1963, which he now displays prominently beneath the glass of his office desk. "It's a memo from J. Edgar Hoover, the first director of the FBI . . . to the attorney general, Robert Kennedy. The memo asked for permission to bug Dr. King—to wiretap him. It's five sentences long and is utterly devoid of factual content. It simply asserts there's a 'communist influence in the racial situation.' There's no date limitation, no geographic limitation. It simply says we need to wiretap this guy."

Rather than challenge Hoover, Kennedy authorized the wiretap, an act later deemed "one of the most ignominious acts in modern American history," according to David Garrow in the *Atlantic*. Indeed, Kennedy's decision—which was made public only five years later, in 1968—dramatically undercut the fragile alliance between the federal government and the black community.

"But here's the hard part," Comey told us. "I have no doubt that those two men believed they were doing the right thing. They were certain the cause was just and certain that their facts were right. And in the absence of constraint and oversight, there was no one to tell them otherwise."

Comey kept the memo beneath the glass on his desk to serve as a reminder of the responsibility the bureau assumes each day. And indeed it's a difficult charge, demanding that the bureau utilize tools meant to ensure Americans' safety without undermining their privacy in the process. Each day, Comey explained, as he reviewed wiretap requests, he couldn't help but glimpse the now notorious Hoover-Kennedy memo. "It is a huge pain in the neck to get permission to bug somebody in the United States," Comey said, "and that's the way it should be. That's constraint. That's oversight. That is power being checked." But far too often—particularly in the Freedom Riders' era—it wasn't.

=====

I arrived at Catherine Burks-Brooks's home later that afternoon. She lives half an hour away from Birmingham, in nearby Center Point, but having grown up in the city, she was well versed in its racial past—including the legacy of the church bombing. Had she been in the wrong place at the wrong time, she might have been a victim herself.

At seventy-six, Catherine has spent a lifetime enduring the brunt of racism in Birmingham and beyond. Her experiences have hardened her, ensuring that she remains a force to be reckoned with—or rather, a force not to be reckoned with. When I first met her a few days earlier at the Freedom Riders' reunion, she told me she would be happy to chat with me—and to set me straight when necessary. I wouldn't be the first writer to require a bit of correction, she assured me, noting two prominent historians whom she previously had to "jump on" to set the record straight. "Sound okay?" she asked.

I gulped and nodded.

Four days later I was knocking on her front door. "Well, come on in now," Catherine said, opening the door wide for me. "Let me show you my museum." I had barely stepped inside before I realized she wasn't joking about the museum. Indeed, her walls are lined with Freedom Rider memorabilia: her mug shot, a photo of her entering a squad car, and several proclamations honoring her and the other Riders. But her museum extended beyond the Freedom Rides. In the living room I spotted a framed poster of Malcolm X, another of Marcus Garvey, and, in between, a few walls dedicated to family photos. Yet my eyes soon drifted to the prints of Egyptian pharaohs. I stopped to study them. "Do the Egyptians hold special meaning for you?" I asked.

"Well, they're my ancestors!" she said, taken aback by my question. "And that's one of the problems right there: our history didn't start with slavery."

"You're right," I agreed, already humbled. "And yet that's where we always start in school."

"I know it is," she affirmed. "And we'd been fighting for about ten thousand years before that."

I moved toward the family photos, listening carefully as Catherine introduced me to her siblings. "And that's me there," she said, pointing to a black-and-white photo of a small girl smiling at the camera. "I was in first grade." Noticing the age gap between her and her siblings, I ask if being the youngest really did help her foster her fighting spirit. "Well," she answered proudly. "I am the only one who ever had that kind of conversation with the Bull." By "that kind" of conversation she meant one both candid and unfiltered, and by "the Bull" she meant Bull Connor, Birmingham's commissioner of public safety from 1937 to 1952 and from 1957 to 1963.

Speaking at First Baptist Church a few nights earlier, Bill Harbour had shared the short version of their midnight right with "the Bull," as well as Catherine's verbal exchange with the man. Now I was eager to hear it from the source. "I had no fear of the Bull," Catherine declared as we took our seats around her dining room table. "And that's why I could talk to the Bull."

"Can you back up?" I asked. "How did this whole nighttime ride take place?"

"We was in jail," Catherine explained. "The Bull had us arrested." Yet the Freedom Riders hadn't been in jail very long before Connor decided that the best course of action was to get them out of his city as soon as possible. In Birmingham Catherine shared a jail cell with fellow Rider Lucretia Collins, a friend from Tennessee A&I. Together they passed the time playing cards with the other inmates in the cell.

But sometime around midnight, long after the card games had wound down, Catherine and Lucretia were jarred awake by a female jailer hollering for them to get dressed, that they were going for a ride. They did as they were told, but when the jailer didn't immediately return, the women assumed the plans had changed, so they removed their clothes and crawled back onto their cots. When the jailer finally returned and found them fast asleep, she began hollering once more, demanding that the women get moving. Begrudgingly, they woke up and dressed again, wholly unaware what the future held for them.

Unbeknownst to Catherine and Lucretia, the men had been given similar instructions, and as the sleepy-eyed Freedom Riders reconvened in the parking lot, they were ushered into a pair of waiting limousines. Catherine was placed on the front bench seat of the leading car, sandwiched between a police deputy and Bull Connor himself.

"What was that ride like?" I pressed. "Was the radio on? Were people nervous?"

"No, the radio was not on," she remembered. "And there was no talking going on in the back."

It was a tense moment for the Riders, particularly because none of them knew just how far Bull Connor was willing to go. Would they be ambushed? Abandoned? Hanged from a tree? What precisely did Bull Connor have planned? While the other Riders appeared visibly nervous, Catherine remained her usual unflappable self. And throughout much of the 120-mile drive from Birmingham to Ardmore, Alabama, Catherine and the Bull chatted. Their subjects ranged from Catherine's frustration about the city's use of tax dollars to fund a new auditorium to Connor's lecture on the formation of the Dixiecrat Party. After a few of the more contentious subjects wound down, Catherine did the unimaginable. "I invited him to join us for breakfast in Nashville," she told me.

"And what'd he say?"

"He said he'd be happy to," Catherine continued. "Of course, ol' Bull never had any intention of taking us all the way to Nashville." As Bill Harbour had explained previously, Connor dropped them off at the Alabama-Tennessee state line instead. The officers tossed the Riders' luggage to the side of the road, and Connor sauntered back to the car.

"Now you know what I told the Bull then, right?" she asked. I shook my head. "I told the Bull we would see him back in Birmingham by high noon," she said. "We watched a lot of cowboy movies in those days, and if something was gonna happen, it was gonna be by high noon."

I couldn't contain my smile. "Of all the stories about the Freedom Rides," I said, "that's got to be one of my favorites." She laughed, and even though she didn't say it aloud, I imagine it was one of her favorites, too. Catherine continued the story I'd heard before: how she, Lucretia Collins, Bill Harbour, John Lewis, and the others wandered the railroad tracks until they stumbled upon a row of houses in the dark. But Catherine added a new detail: they came upon several homes, and it was up to the Riders to decide which house was most likely to take them in.

"We could tell the difference between where black people lived and where white folks lived, because usually houses on one side of the track is black and houses on the other side is white," Catherine explained. "And that's how we determined who was who. And we were right." It's a good thing, because as the Riders knew all too well, a knock on the wrong door might have led to a far different result.

Years later she learned that only six black families lived in that particular section of town, a further reminder of how lucky they were that night. But luck was only part of it, Catherine noted. After they knocked on the shack door and found the man inside less than welcoming, Catherine relied upon a lesson she'd learned from her mother. "Whenever you want something done," Catherine told me, "you talk to the woman of the house." And that is exactly what they did. At Catherine's urging, the Riders knocked once more, and this time they directed their plea to the woman who lived there. "She said, 'Let them children in here,'" Catherine recalled. "I can still almost hear the locks coming off that door."

"Did you see her at that point?" I asked.

"No. I just heard her voice."

"But her husband obeyed?"

"Oh yeah." Catherine smiled. "He obeyed."

═══

Sometimes disobedience was a workable strategy, particularly when done with civility. Indeed, civil disobedience played a role throughout the Freedom Rides, though not in the way many expected. Civil disobedience refers to the intentional *breaking* of laws considered to be unjust, yet when the Freedom Riders boarded the interstate buses, they were actually *obeying* the law. The Supreme Court's *Morgan v. Virginia* and *Boynton v. Virginia* rulings had confirmed it. At their worst, the Freedom Riders were mostly "disobedient" rule followers—if such a thing exists. When they were arrested, for instance, it wasn't for riding the buses, it was for breach of the peace—a convenient excuse for local law enforcement to reach for their handcuffs.

Occasionally some Freedom Riders proved to be "disobedient" even among their own ranks. On the afternoon of Sunday, May 14, 1961, Catherine, Jim Zwerg, Bill Harbour, and several other members of the Nashville Student Movement were picnicking when they received word of the ill-fated violence directed toward the first wave of Freedom Riders. "It was like going back in the service, I suppose," Catherine told me. The Nashville Student Movement participants had just completed their integration of the movie theaters, and already they were being called back to duty, this time on a different front.

Within minutes of hearing the news, Catherine and the others returned to headquarters to begin planning their response. As Catherine noted, the group was in complete agreement that the Freedom Rides should continue; it was simply a matter of how to proceed, as well as who would come along. As their plans began to solidify, Diane Nash placed calls to several of the movement's leaders, including Dr. King of the SCLC and James Farmer of CORE, both of whom urged her to reconsider. On the surface the Nashville Student Movement's plan to continue the Ride appeared reckless, naive, and all but certain to brew further hostilities. What was the point? some wondered. And what would it serve to accomplish?

Yet Nash and the other Nashville students believed that the Ride's continuation was critical, and thus they disobeyed—or at least disregarded—the advice bestowed upon them by senior members of the movement. And so, on the morning of May 17, the youthful Nashville coalition boarded the buses without their elders' blessings.

After this "disobedience," the rule following began. Catherine remembered the trip from Birmingham to Montgomery as orderly, pleasant, and uneventful—so uneventful, in fact, that Catherine, like John Lewis, even managed to squeeze in a nap. "For some reason I woke up just as we got to the city limits," Catherine recalled. And as she did, she watched as their trooper escort suddenly veered away, leaving them vulnerable. She peered out the window, anxious for the Montgomery police to take over the rest of the route, but the squad cars never appeared.

"When we got to the bus station everything was calm and quiet," she said, leaning forward across the table. "I didn't hardly see anyone. But about five minutes later all hell broke loose. People just came from everywhere." They streamed in from the sides of the building and across the street, marching with weapons clenched in their fists. The Riders had nowhere to run and nowhere to hide, and as the mob closed in, the best they could do was heed John Lewis's call to circle in tight.

Jim Zwerg and John Lewis stood with blood running down their faces; William Barbee fell to the ground, and the newspaper reporters and photojournalists fell next to him. "I could hear the white women screaming," Catherine said. "And they had babies in their arms, but they kept screaming, 'Kill them niggers, kill them niggers.'"

Catherine, Lucretia Collins, Susan Wilbur, and Susan Hermann hustled away from the station as quickly as they could, searching frantically for an escape. Eventually they flagged down a cab, and the women piled inside, unaware of the Alabama law that prevented the black cabbie from driving Susan Wilbur and Susan Hermann, both of whom were white. When the driver refused to go, in the heat of the moment Catherine made an executive decision for all of them. "Fine," she said, hauling herself back onto the street. "If they can't go, then we don't go."

With few options remaining, the women prepared themselves for whatever might come. And what came, according to Catherine, was Bernard LaFayette, who urged the black women back into the cab and promised to do his best to find another way out for the white women. With Bernard's assurance, Catherine relented, and she and Lucretia piled back into the cab. But even then the cabbie was afraid to drive them. "Get out," Catherine ordered him. "Let me drive." A few years earlier Catherine's father had taught her the basics of driving a car with an automatic transmission, but she had never learned to drive a stick shift—now quite a problem, given that the cab happened to have one. Upon learning of this complication, the women began pleading with the driver once more, reminding him that the mob was heading their way.

As the mob began maneuvering to cut off their escape, Catherine eyed the only exit that remained—going the wrong way on a one-way street— and pointed the driver toward it. The driver refused. What if something was to happen to the cab? "Look, you go down this one-way street," Catherine ordered, "and if something happens to this cab, the SCLC will pay for it." Catherine certainly didn't hold the purse strings of the Southern Christian Leadership Conference, but she figured a monetary guarantee from the SCLC held more weight than one from the cash-strapped students from Nashville. "Just take us to a black community and drop us off," she pleaded.

Finally the driver relented. As the cab squealed away, Catherine turned to see the blood running down Zwerg's and Lewis's faces. She watched, horrified, as the fists continued their relentless pummeling. She was helpless, but she was safe, which was a far better predicament than that of the men left behind on the sidewalk.

=====

Fifty-five years removed from that moment I wondered, where had the FBI been? In fact, agents had been there, but they had been limited to an observational role. And so they observed from close range as fists slammed into Jim Zwerg's head and a pipe cracked William Barbee's head. They made phone calls and wrote reports, but at no point did they intervene.

This was the FBI's strategy before the Civil Rights Act of 1964. After the May 14 beating at the Trailways station in Birmingham, Attorney General Kennedy began questioning the sincerity of the FBI's role. "Although Robert Kennedy never knew the full extent of the FBI's advance knowledge of the Alabama plot," wrote historian Raymond Arsenault, "he and other Justice Department officials suspected that the FBI was partly responsible for the crisis. After all, it was no secret that J. Edgar Hoover was a racial conservative who firmly believed that the civil rights movement was riddled with Communist sympathizers."

Indeed, it wasn't a secret. And, as Arsenault confirmed, Hoover's personal feelings on the subject of civil rights surely informed his professional duties. Nevertheless, it seemed inconceivable to me that the FBI could witness crimes being committed in broad daylight just a stone's throw away and still refuse to intervene. To gain a better perspective of the FBI's history with civil rights, I went to the source: FBI historian John Fox. In a phone interview Dr. Fox confirmed what I had already gleaned to be true: before the Civil Rights Act, our country's civil rights laws, as he put it, "did not have a whole lot of teeth to them."

"Over the years the bureau would investigate a number of cases—if there was a lynching on government property, of course we'd have a responsibility to investigate . . . so we *did* investigate them," he stressed. "But as far as racially motivated civil rights violations went, the bureau's take, to some extent, was 'We don't have a whole lot of authority here.'"

Even as it began to gain authority, the FBI hardly relished its new role. It was but one more wrinkle in an already messy business, and hardly Hoover's top priority. "Hoover's bureau was powerful because Hoover was a leader who really liked to have boundaries," Fox explained, adding that civil rights violations made Hoover's preestablished boundaries become a bit more porous.

"In the case of the Freedom Riders," Fox continued, "you're dealing with a couple of different issues." But the main issue involved jurisdiction as the Riders traveled from state to state. Hoover believed that protecting individuals from violence was a local matter, not a federal matter. "And so what they ended up doing, largely," Fox said, "was watching."

In retrospect, the FBI's lackluster efforts on behalf of the Freedom Riders is indeed disappointing, further proof of the kind of inaction that contributed to what James Comey described as the "disconnect between communities and law enforcement officers." The director's words still rang in my ears: "We were late to this fight." They certainly were. Hoover had made sure of it.

=====

As my conversation with Catherine wound down, I leafed through a few papers until I came across a photograph of her mug shot. There she was at twenty-one, in a collared shirt and a cardigan sweater, an unmistakable smirk on her face. "What was going through your head when they took that shot?" I asked, the same question I had asked Mimi Feingold several months earlier. "What were you thinking?"

Catherine took the photo in her hands and studied herself for a while. "I was just tired and ready to go to sleep. I didn't even fix my collar up or anything. My hair just—look at that," she said, shaking her head. "I knew I was going to jail, and I knew I was getting a floor or a top bunk, and I was ready for that. I didn't even know I had a smirk on. I just wanted to go to sleep."

I nodded. Although my own journey didn't compare to hers, I admitted that I too was beginning to feel worn down. "I was talking to a Freedom Rider the other night over at First Baptist Church," I said. "And he told me he was afraid that your generation had dropped the torch—that the Freedom Riders, in particular, didn't tell the story as well as you might have, and that as a result the younger generation doesn't understand. Is that your take, too?"

"I often say that's what we did," she agreed. "We didn't stress it enough. A number of us were too busy working to get our ends to meet, and we didn't talk to the young people about it. Not just about what we did, but what *needs* to be done and what *can* be done."

"What can be done?" I asked. "What can a guy like me do?" She gave me a smirk reminiscent of the one in her mug shot. "It's okay," I told her. "I can take it."

"A guy like you," she declared, "he can tell the story."

Five minutes later I was walking down her front steps, more motivated than ever to do just that. As I slipped into the car, I thought back to the night fifty-five years ago when Catherine had taken her seat directly beside Bull Connor. "It is hard," FBI Director Comey had said, "to hate up close."

It makes a good theory, at least.

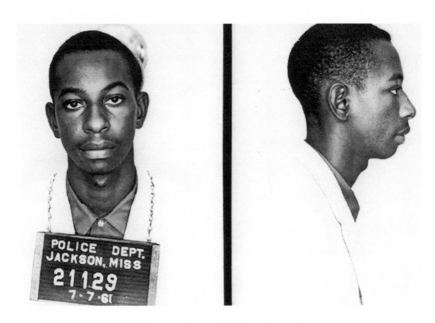

Figure 9. Hezekiah Watkins, mug shot, July 7, 1961.

Mississippi State Sovereignty Commission, "Mississippi State Sovereignty Commission Photograph," July 7, 1961, SCRID# 2-55-5-76-1-1-1ph, Series 2515: Mississippi State Sovereignty Commission Records, 1994–2006, Mississippi Department of Archives and History, February 20, 2017, http://mdah.ms.gov/arrec/digital_archives/sovcom/photo.php?display=item&oid=248.

8

Hezekiah Watkins

Jackson, Mississippi

"My mother, preacher, principal, teachers, they was all preaching, 'If those Freedom Riders come here, don't y'all get involved.' They began to tell us things that could happen if you did—things that could happen to you, to your mother, to your house, to your job, to everybody."

My journey was supposed to end with a trip to Parchman Farm—my attempt to conclude my ride where the original Freedom Riders had concluded theirs. I had been planning my visit for months, undergoing a background check, then negotiating the terms of my visit with frequent phone calls to various prison representatives. I prodded, begged, and cut through all the red tape I could. Months passed, the bureaucratic machine trudged on, and a mere forty-eight hours before my tentative visit date, there was still no guarantee I would be let inside.

A few hours after my conversation with Catherine Burks-Brooks, I at last received a call informing me that my visit had been canceled: the prison was in the process of reviewing their lockdown procedures, and they refused to allow me to visit until that work was complete. I was devastated, frustrated, and a little bit angry, too. The only way to visit Parchman, it seemed, was to be convicted of a crime.

But the prison was right to cancel my visit. I learned later that in the days leading up to my arrival, five prison staff members had been assaulted by inmates—hence the need for the review. Still, I couldn't help but feel personally betrayed. I had traveled thousands of miles, after all, and now my journey was being cut short because of forces beyond my control.

For the first time on my entire trip, I felt lost. Having covered all those miles in all those days, I simply didn't know where the road might lead me next. All I knew was that I had booked a couple of nonrefundable nights at a hotel in Jackson, Mississippi, so I had a bit of time on my hands. Although I was looking forward to my final interview with Freedom Rider Hezekiah Watkins, beyond that my schedule was now far too free for my liking.

In the midst of my funk I wandered around the Jackson streets, walking block after block in search of something. And then I found just the something I was looking for: the office of the *Clarion-Ledger*. I paused before the imposing building, sorting through my mental Rolodex until I pulled up a name: Jerry Mitchell, an award-winning investigative reporter I had heard speak several years ago while I was in graduate school. Jerry's reporting, I remembered, had played a major role in reopening several civil rights cold cases, bringing criminals to justice decades after their crimes. Most notable were Jerry's reports on Byron De La Beckwith, the murderer of Medgar Evers, Mississippi's NAACP field secretary; thirty-one years after pulling the trigger, the Klansman was at last successfully prosecuted.

I was feeling bold, so I ran back to my hotel room, tracked down Jerry's contact information, and sent him an email out of the blue. "I know you're busy," I wrote, "but if you have a few minutes . . ." Five minutes later my phone rang. "You want to grab dinner at the Mayflower Café?" Jerry asked. Five minutes later we did. I had just settled into a booth in the café when in walked fifty-seven-year-old Jerry, clad in khakis, a dress shirt, and a Dr. Seuss necktie. He eased into the seat across from me with the confidence of a man who holds the key to the city, which he pretty much did. Everyone in Jackson knew Jerry, and Jerry knew everyone, too. But his reputation extended well beyond the city. In 2009 Jerry was a MacArthur "Genius Grant" recipient, further solidifying his reputation as one of the best investigative journalists around.

You wouldn't know any of this by his casual demeanor, however. "So what brings you to Jackson?" he asked, reaching for a packet of crackers. I told him about my failed effort to visit Parchman and noted my upcoming interview with a local Freedom Rider. "Who's that?" he asked.

"Hezekiah Watkins."

"Oh sure." Jerry nodded. "He and I've done a few speaking engagements together. He'll tell you a good story."

I didn't doubt it. But at the moment the story I most wanted to hear was Jerry's—in particular, how he got murder suspects to open up to him. "What's the secret?" I inquired. "How do you get people like Byron De La Beckwith to talk to you?"

"Well, I try to go talk to them," he said simply.

"You just—talk to them?"

"Oh yeah," he said offhandedly, folding a cracker into his mouth. "I go sit in their house, just go talk to them. I do it all the time."

"But *how* do you get them to talk to you?"

"Sometimes I say, 'Hey, this is what people are saying. Of course, I want to get your side of it.'"

"Like you're doing them a favor?" I asked.

"Yeah, that's basically how I do it."

The conversation soon turned directly to Beckwith—a far cry from the Freedom Rides, but a story I still needed to know. I had seen the Hollywood portrayal, of course, but I want to know the nuts and bolts, the details, and, if possible, pick up a few reporting tips in the process.

It all started with the Mississippi State Sovereignty Commission, Jerry explained, a state agency that from 1956 to 1977 saw its mission as being to "protect the sovereignty of the state of Mississippi and her sister states" from "federal encroachment." It did so primarily by surveillance, intelligence, and public relations—a three-pronged approach to the growing civil rights "problem" that "plagued" the state. In its efforts to "protect," the Sovereignty Commission created files on tens of thousands of people connected to the civil rights movement, including a file on the assassination of Medgar Evers. At the commission's closure in 1977, the Mississippi legislature voted to seal the files for fifty years, a move that confirmed for Jerry the importance of the information inside.

Throughout the 1980s the *Clarion-Ledger* received about twenty-four hundred pages of leaks from those files, a treasure trove that Jerry dubbed "the Sovereignty Commission's greatest hits." He explained, "We started reporting what was in them and did a big package of stories. One of them was about the [1964] Evers [trial]. What it showed was that while one arm of the state [had been] prosecuting Byron De La Beckwith, the other arm of the state—the Sovereignty Commission—[had been] secretly assisting the defense in trying to get Beckwith acquitted."

Jerry broke that story in October 1989, prompting Myrlie Evers, Medgar's widow, to press city officials to reopen the case. By the end of that month the district attorney had done just that. Around the same time Jerry had managed to track down Beckwith to his rural, off-grid home in Signal Mountain, Tennessee. "He lived in this wooden house," Jerry remembered. "It was up on a hill. The way you go up there is on this winding, curvy road. I felt like I was going into *Deliverance* or something."

He arrived midafternoon, and for the next six hours he listened as Beckwith ranted about his troubles with black people. Hours later, with his notebook filled, Jerry thanked Beckwith for taking the time, then stood up to leave. "It was starting to get dark," Jerry said, "and he insisted on walking me out to the car. I was like, 'Really, that's okay. I think I can handle it.' He walked me out anyway."

The pair stepped outside into the evening, and as Jerry reached for the door of his car, Beckwith offered a warning: "If you write positive things about white Caucasian Christians, then God will bless you. If you write negative things about white Caucasian Christians, God will punish you. And if God does not punish you," he added ominously, "then several individuals will do it for him."

Months later, when Beckwith found himself once more in a Mississippi courtroom—in part because of Jerry's articles—he narrowed his eyes and turned to the nearest reporter. "You see that boy over there?" he hollered, pointing to Jerry. "When he dies he's going to Africa!"

Upon hearing this, Jerry turned to his friends and said, "You know, I've always wanted to go!"

I couldn't help but chuckle. It was a rare moment of levity amid the madness. "I still can't believe you just knocked on his door," I said.

"I can't believe it, either," Jerry stated, laughing. "I'm in the midst of writing this book, and I'm revisiting what I've done, and I think, man, I can't believe some of the things I did when I was younger."

"Because it was crazy?"

"Yeah, because it was crazy." He smiled. "I just walked right in: 'Hey Byron De La Beckwith, I want to talk to you.'"

"Well, you gotta get the story," I said with a shrug.

"That's exactly it," he agreed, nodding as the waitress delivered his cup of gumbo. "You *gotta* get the story."

=====

Two days later I knocked on Hezekiah Watkins's front door—my last chance to get the Freedom Riders' story as best I can. It was eight o'clock in the morning, but the sixty-eight-year-old was already wide-awake. He gripped my hand tight and welcomed me into his home. "Come in, come in," he said. "You want coffee?" Eight days into my journey, I was in no position to turn that down.

We sat next to each other on his expansive couch while a sports highlight reel played on the big TV screen in front of us. "Tell me about your trip," he said, so I did, describing my time with Bernard LaFayette, Bill Harbour, and Catherine Burks-Brooks, and others. "You," I concluded, "are my last interview."

"Saving the best for last, huh?" He grinned.

"I guess we'll see," I said, smiling as I reached for my pen.

Hezekiah was born in Milwaukee, Wisconsin, in 1947, and before he was two he had moved with his mother to her former home in Rankin County, Mississippi. Eight years later they moved to nearby Hinds County, leaving their rural home for the state capital. "When we moved to Jackson, man, I thought we was rich," Hezekiah said, shaking his head. "Rankin was a very small community, but in Jackson, not only did we have running water, we had hot and cold water. We had indoor plumbing—a bathtub where you could take a bath. We had so many things that was so exciting to me, things I'd only witnessed on TV."

Although indoor plumbing did indeed change his life, perhaps the greatest change came as a result of his new friends, several of whom were white. In those days, Hezekiah explained, Jackson's black and white residents were primarily divided by nothing more than the east and west sides of Lamar Street. "We could stand in our backyard and wave to the white kids, and they'd stand in their front yard and wave at us," he recalled. And that is exactly what they did.

Eventually those waves grew into conversations, and those conversations grew into marble-shooting tournaments—the kids' pastime of choice. After school, while their parents were still at work, Hezekiah and several other school-age black children from the west side of Lamar journeyed to a grass-less patch of land on the east side. The grassless area was perfect for shoot-ing marbles, and even though it extended down both sides of the street, it took awhile before the white children began venturing to the west side.

The street itself was hardly a barrier, but what it represented most cer-tainly was. Economically, Hezekiah believed, black and white residents in that area were on equal footing ("They were just as poor as we were"), but the racial disparity remained an omnipresent force up and down that street—at least when adults were around. However, the children always remained civil, even in the midst of a high-stakes game of marbles. "I can never remember a fight. Not even an argument," Hezekiah said. "Seriously. We got along well."

Hezekiah smiled as he recalled those long hot afternoons shooting marbles with his new friends. "Those white kids hadn't been taught bigotry or hatred yet," he noted. "But the older they got, that's when they started to learn it. Eventually they just stopped playing in the yard and stopped waving. When they learned what the deal was, they just went off to their side and never did make it back."

"So you didn't really experience racism firsthand until after your marble-shooting days?" I asked.

Hezekiah mulled over my question. "I'm going to put it to you like this," he replied. "It was just a way of life. We knew what we could and couldn't do. It was embedded in us all along."

"So there was no first experience with racism," I amended. "You were always experiencing it."

"Exactly. You'd experience racism on a daily, hourly, minute, second basis every day." It was expected, he explained. It was protocol.

During their early-morning walks to school, Hezekiah and his black friends were often pelted with objects hurled by the white children from their bus windows. In addition to throwing objects, the white kids often slung a few racial slurs. "Of course, as children, we'd pick up rocks and throw them back at the bus." Hezekiah laughed. "We didn't think a lot about it because the kids on the buses would be laughing, and we'd all be laughing, and when the bus got out of our reach it was back to whatever we were talking about."

"It was—a game?"

"Well, it was nothing that lingered on," he said. "It happened this second, and the next second everything was okay."

"The kids who threw things at you," I continued, "were they the same kids you shot marbles with?"

He took a sip of coffee before answering. "You know," he replied at last, "I can't really say they were." But he couldn't say they weren't, either.

———

Throughout the summer of 1961, Hezekiah remained glued to his mother's television set, watching the nightly news with growing horror as the Freedom Riders were beaten, bombed, and eventually arrested right in his hometown of Jackson—their final stop before Parchman. The thirteen-year-old adjusted the TV antenna as best he could, cupping aluminum foil over the top of the rabbit ears to eke out a bit more clarity. But all that clarity ever revealed was violence, and it roused within him such admiration for the

Riders that one night in early July Hezekiah and his buddy Troy headed over to a mass meeting at a nearby Masonic temple in the hope of seeing a few.

By the time they arrived the rally had wound down. However, upon hearing the rumor that a busload of Riders was going to arrive soon at the Greyhound station, they immediately hustled over to catch a glimpse. At first they awaited the Riders' arrival from a safe distance across the street, but their view was so obscured that Troy suggested they head over to the station for a closer look.

Hezekiah agreed, running across Lamar Street while Troy trotted just a few steps behind. "So we get to the door of the bus station," Hezekiah explained, "and Troy *pushed* me inside. Now, if Troy was here, he would tell you what he's been saying all his life: that he was *pulling* me backward, trying to keep me from entering. But I'm here to tell you"—Hezekiah stopped to chuckle—"that Troy pushed me *inside* that station."

According to Hezekiah, it was Troy's push that thrust him into the fray at the bus station, putting him at risk. The Jackson police took one look at the new arrival and immediately pegged him as a Freedom Rider. It didn't matter that Hezekiah lived just a few blocks away. For the officers present that night, he fit the Freedom Rider description perfectly: he was young, he was black, and he was there. And within moments he was ordered to stand against the wall.

"I was scared to shit, you hear me?" Hezekiah told me. "My mother, preacher, principal, teachers, they was all preaching, 'If those Freedom Riders come here, don't y'all get involved.' They began to tell us things that could happen if you did—things that could happen to you, to your mother, to your house, to your job, to everybody."

"Like what?" I asked, although I suspected I knew at least a few of the answers.

"Number one: your house could be burned. Or your mom could be taken and beaten and raped. The Klan was doing all of these things back then." And these were the very acts of retribution that ran through his mind as the police officer headed his way.

"Name?" the officer demanded.

"Hezekiah Watkins."

"Place of birth?"

"Milwaukee, Wisconsin."

The officer looked at him, nodding slowly. "Okay, okay."

"But I didn't know what 'okay' meant," Hezekiah told me. "All I knew was that I'd come there wanting to see what a Freedom Rider looked like." And now, inadvertently, he had become one.

Confused, Hezekiah remained mum while being loaded into the paddy wagon. He was tired, scared, and suddenly alone (since Troy had gotten away). And as the miles passed it became increasingly clear that he wasn't being hauled off to the Jackson City Jail. Peering out the peepholes, all he saw was darkness, broken only occasionally by the shimmer of headlights passing them from the opposite direction. "We took a long, long ride late that night," Hezekiah said, his voice softening. "And when I get out of the paddy wagon—I don't have no idea of the time, we're just going to say two or three o'clock in the morning—they walked me across a yard, and I remember thinking to myself how well kept that yard was."

It wasn't until after dawn that he learned that the well-kept yard was his new home: Parchman Farm. Pulled from the paddy wagon, he was placed in a cell with two sleeping men. "They was murderers," Hezekiah found out, and "rapists." After a restless sleep that night, he awoke the following morning to find his cellmates studying him. "What you doing up here?" one asked. "You mighty young to be here."

"I don't know," thirteen-year-old Hezekiah replied nervously. "I'm just—here."

"Yeah, right," one of the men chuckled. "I'm just here, too." The men began interrogating him further—"Where you from? What'd they charge you with?"—until one of his cellmates drew his own conclusion. "I know why you're here," the man said. "You raped a white woman."

Hezekiah's eyes bulged at the unfounded accusation.

"Yeah, that's it," the man repeated. "They're gonna hang your ass. They're gonna string you up, man."

"But I didn't do nothing," Hezekiah protested.

"Well, you must've done *something*," the man said, "cuz you're on death row."

Hezekiah mulled the words over in his head. "Death? Row?" he asked. "What is death row?"

The man laughed. "You're on it."

─────

Throughout Hezekiah's three days or so on death row, his mother tried desperately to find him, well aware of the fate that occasionally befell black boys who disappeared in Mississippi. "She didn't have no idea where I was,"

Hezekiah said. "She just knew her child was missing. And Troy, who lived right across the street, he was scared to say anything because he knew if he told my mom what had happened, then his mom would've killed him."

Although Troy remained quiet, Hezekiah didn't. When he informed the prison guards that he was thirteen years old, the prison officials, apparently horrified at the notion of having a minor in their possession, ordered his immediate release. "Governor Barnett was a racist SOB," Hezekiah said, referring the Mississippi's governor at the time. "I don't know whether he didn't want the publicity, or he thought something would happen to me, or whatever, but I'm told that he told the prison to release me right away. They put me in that same paddy wagon and drove me right on back to Jackson." Yet before releasing him, the Jackson Police Department first demanded a mug shot of the young boy. Fifty-five years later, I handed him a copy. "Yeah, that's me," he admitted, laughing.

"That's a nice suit coat," I observed, commenting on his mug shot. "That's what you wore the night you were arrested?"

"Apparently so," he said. "Because I never had a chance to change." And it was the same suit coat he wore when his mother at last retrieved him from the Jackson jail.

"What'd your mother say when you reunited?" I ask.

"My mother was very, very glad to see me." He smiled. "And then she whipped the hell out of me."

———

Although that July night at the Jackson Greyhound station was Hezekiah's first arrest, it was hardly his last. "I'm told I was arrested over a hundred times," he stated. "But I don't know how true that is."

At thirteen, Hezekiah had no intention of earning such a rap sheet for his civil rights protests, and in fact he might not have joined the movement at all had it not been for the recruitment efforts of James Bevel. Bevel, one of the leaders of the Nashville Student Movement, earned his civil rights stripes over the years through a number of demonstrations. From Bevel's time on the Freedom Rides to his later work as the SCLC's director of direct action, his commitment to the cause is well-known. Despite his many positive attributes, on occasion some considered him defiant, uncompromising, and persistent to a fault—all attributes Hezekiah witnessed firsthand. Bevel had also been incarcerated in Parchman, and upon being released in July 1961 he decided to stick around Jackson to begin his own recruitment efforts in the area. Hezekiah, the thirteen-year-old Freedom Rider, was very much on his radar.

One day while his mother was at work, Hezekiah heard a knock on his door. He answered it to find a smiling James Bevel standing before him. "Of all the folks in Jackson," I inquired, "why'd he knock on your door?"

"Because he wanted me to try to get other young blacks involved in the movement," Hezekiah said. "And he knew that I could help." Hezekiah recalled Bevel making nearly daily visits to his home throughout much of 1962. "He worked on me for about a year after my first arrest," Hezekiah recalled. "But I didn't want no part in it."

Eventually, though, Bevel's persistence paid off. One day, after many long conversations about the importance of their shared fight for equality, Hezekiah agreed to accompany Bevel on a bus trip to observe racial inequalities occurring right there in Jackson. They had hardly stepped foot on the bus before those inequalities were immediately brought to light. Hezekiah paid his fare and started toward the back of the bus, as usual, when Bevel stopped him and urged him to take a seat up front with him. "No, man," Hezekiah replied nervously, "we got to sit in the back."

Saving the battle for another day, Bevel relented, allowing his protégé to return to the back of the bus where he had always sat. But already Hezekiah's eyes were opening to the problems that plagued his city, and their tour was only beginning. "So we walked downtown together," Hezekiah continued, "and he showed me the water fountain that I had to drink from, and then we walked past Woolworth's and he showed me where I had to go to order a burger or whatever. He showed me all the things I couldn't see. I mean, I knew it was always there, but until James put it right before me like that, I never really saw it. It was like a veil coming off."

Despite this eye-opening experience, Hezekiah still remained unwilling to commit himself fully to the cause. He was worried about his mother's job and personal safety—neither of which he was willing to risk to placate some outside agitator. "But he kept on every day," Hezekiah stated. "He said, 'We need you. *I* need you.'"

Eventually, James tried another tactic: realizing that the key to winning over Hezekiah was to win over his mother first. "James was a preacher, and my mom was a religious fanatic," Hezekiah explained. "So he started coming over some evenings to read the Bible with my mother. And that blew my mom's mind. So one day my mom invited him to church, and he went. He asked the minister if he could give the message, and the minister said yes.

So James got up and did some preaching. When we came back to the house and had dinner, that's when James began talking to my mother about letting me join the movement. Finally, my mother said, 'Okay, if you promise to protect my son and not let anything happen to him.'" James agreed. And despite the dozens of arrests that followed, he stayed true to his word.

"There were no fathers in my neighborhood," Hezekiah noted. "And I mean zero. I can look back right now and see all of the houses where I grew up, and there wasn't a father in any of those houses." For Hezekiah and other young African Americans in Jackson, James Bevel served as a surrogate of sorts. "He was the person I was looking up to. He was the man who had the knowledge. He was *the* man. I know I shouldn't say this but James Bevel, in my mind, was more powerful than Dr. King."

For Hezekiah, Bevel was certainly a more constant presence. Although Hezekiah marched alongside Dr. King, and on occasion shared a large cell with him in Jackson, their relationship was not nearly as close as the one he shared with James. "I was his lieutenant," Hezekiah reported, "because I brought other kids in. Based on me, he was able to convert them to the movement. Although we mainly discussed civil rights issues, he also taught me a lot in terms of becoming a man."

There was one instance, Hezekiah remembered, when his lesson was particularly piercing. After a protest in which one demonstrator was severely beaten by police, Bevel, Hezekiah, and the other recently arrested demonstrators began angrily pacing around their Jackson City Jail cell. The beating had left the others fiery and anxious for revenge. Although Bevel understood the importance of nonviolence as a strategy, he had made clear to Hezekiah that he hadn't adopted it as a way of life. And in the aftermath of yet another beating of a black man at the hands of police, he'd had enough. From inside the jail cell, Hezekiah, Bevel, and several others began singing "I'm Gonna Do What the Spirit Say Do," a freedom song that occasionally lent itself to an improvisational verse or two. In the jail cell that day, a fired-up Bevel hurled an unexpected—and explicit—verse into the void: "I'll fuck 'em up, if the spirit says fuck," he howled. "I'll fuck 'em up, if the spirit says fuck."

"This was a preacher singing," Hezekiah stressed, "and it shocked all of us." The others soon joined in, their rage intensifying along with their profanity. "It was like we was high on something," Hezekiah said. "We were ready to *do* something. When I think back, I'm glad the police officers didn't come into our cell during that time. We were so hyped right then that this nonviolent stuff didn't seem too important."

For the next several years Hezekiah's commitment to the movement continued to grow, reaching a fever pitch of sorts on June 11, 1963—just hours after Governor George Wallace's infamous Stand in the Schoolhouse Door at the University of Alabama, his theatrical attempt to deny qualified black students the right to their education. After Governor Wallace stood down at the behest of the National Guard, the people of Jackson began preparing for a demonstration of their own. That very night, NAACP Field Secretary Medgar Evers was scheduled to speak at a church in Jackson, and Hezekiah had been enlisted to assist with security. "Here," one of the higher-ups said, handing Hezekiah a .22-caliber pistol. "Keep an eye on the perimeter."

"I was about sixteen," Hezekiah told me. "Was I going to use it? I didn't know. But I had it. It was in my pocket while I was riding my bicycle." That night Hezekiah remained on high alert, but he never sensed so much as a whiff of danger. He never caught a glimpse of Medgar Evers, either—and in fact he never would again. At a few minutes past midnight on June 12, 1963, while Evers was returning to his home on Guynes Street, Byron De La Beckwith fired a single bullet into Evers's heart, and he fell in his carport. He was a World War II veteran, a survivor of the Normandy invasion, but back in the United States he couldn't avoid being murdered on his own property.

"I felt as though I was—not to blame for his assassination, but a little responsible," Hezekiah remembered. After all, for a few hours that night, Hezekiah was one of the only people standing between Medgar Evers and a bullet. And shortly after Hezekiah's security detail ended, so too did Evers's life.

Ten minutes after leaving Hezekiah's home, I parked my car in front of Medgar Evers's house, peering out the window at the modest, one-story ranch directly before me. I exited the car to read the historical marker in front of the house, to refresh myself on the details I mostly already knew. The marker said that Evers, "Mississippi's first NAACP Field Secretary," had served as an "outspoken activist for voter registration and social justice." It cost him his life.

Yet on the subject of the Freedom Riders, Evers had remained less than supportive. In fact, upon receiving advance notice of the proposed Ride, Evers informed James Farmer that the Freedom Riders' visit to Jackson would serve as an unnecessary distraction. "As much as we would like to be of help," Evers wrote, "we feel that CORE's coming into Jackson at this time on a sponsored trip for the purpose stated in your letter will not have the effect intended and will possibly hamper some of the efforts already in progress."

Clarifying his message further, Evers suggested that "it would perhaps be better for you to by pass [sic] Mississippi and proceed to your destination." This was hardly the welcome CORE had hoped for, but Evers had his own initiatives to consider. And as a resident of Jackson, he arguably had the clearer view of the unintended consequences the Freedom Riders might bring to his city, despite their good intentions.

We all bring our baggage; certainly I had mine. If I had avoided feeling like a "tragedy tourist" back at the 16th Street Baptist Church, there was no avoiding it now. At the moment, I fit the description perfectly: a white guy from the North loitering around an assassinated black man's front yard. I hoped to better understand Medgar Evers's story—to try to hold the heaviness of history for a while—but I knew how this must look. In the house directly to my left, I spotted an elderly woman in a nightgown glancing at me through her window. Later I learned that she had lived in that house for more than fifty years and was present the night Evers was shot.

That information came courtesy of Minnie Watson, an archivist at nearby Tougaloo College who had agreed to give me a tour this morning. She pulled up at the side of the road, and I introduced myself, thanking her for taking the time. "No problem," she said, "just give me a moment to set up." I loitered in the yard for a few more minutes and watched Minnie enter the house, open the curtains, and flick on the lights. "Okay," she said at last, "come on in."

I entered through the door that led from the carport to the living room—the same door Evers was going to use on the night he was killed. I stepped inside, and Minnie began her brief tour, starting with the living room window where a bullet tore through and ending with the wall that still retains a bullethole. She told me what it was like being a student at a mass meeting when Evers took to the mic, the way she and the rest of the crowd turned electric as Evers preached to them about the importance of joining the NAACP.

After ten minutes of chatting, Minnie encouraged me to see the rest of the house for myself. "We've got some placards in the room on the right there," she pointed out. I thanked her, then dedicated another fifteen minutes or so to wandering from one room to the next. I peered inside bedroom closets and bathroom drawers—my attempt to find an answer to the question I can't ask: how a man kills another man in cold blood, and in front of the victim's family, no less.

The story of Medgar Evers has more than its fair share of immeasurable sadness: Evers's insistence that the architect raise the windows in his children's room to ensure that no stray bullets would find them, and his further insistence that the house be built without a front door—a change in design that he hoped might keep his family safe. The side door was much safer, he believed, since the carport would provide a bit more cover—though not enough, as he learned in the early hours of June 12.

Medgar Evers became a martyr, and his legend lives on. Minnie shared several stories about him, opening my eyes to him as a husband, a father, and apparently a soothsayer, too. Minnie told me how on the day of Evers's death, his wife, Myrlie, asked about ironing a few of his shirts for him, to which he replied, "I won't need them." Had he sensed his own impending death? Or did he simply live in a time and place where a black man never quite knew which breath might be his last?

Minnie waited in the living room as I entered the Everses' bedroom. I rested my hands on the dresser and peered at myself in the mirror. Then I made my way to the children's bedroom; it resembles my own children's bedroom, except for the raised windows and lower beds.

Medgar Evers was many things: a husband, a father, a soldier, and a field secretary, but most of all he was simply a human being—one who went to work each day knowing he might not come back, and one who, just like the Freedom Riders, understood the risks and acted in spite of them.

After the tour of the house, Minnie walked me back to the carport, where a bloodstain still remains. She showed me the steps toward which Evers crawled in the moments after he had been shot. Then she pointed to the place across the street from where the bullet had been fired. She showed me everything, told me everything, and filled my mind and heart with more than I thought they could bear. "Now then," she concluded, "any questions?"

=====

Sometimes we northerners forget it, but history hangs heavy in the South. There, below the Mason-Dixon line, you can hardly walk down a street without spotting a historical marker. And if you're like me, you'd probably stop to read every one. This explains why, during my four-year stint in Alabama, my round-the-block dog walks were interminable. I was curious about every name on every last marker, and my poor dog paid the price. How many names did I scrawl into my notebook? How many people from the past did I desperately try to know?

During my last afternoon in Jackson, I returned to my historical-marker proclivities. But this time, for the first time, I was too emotionally exhausted to even write down the names. After my morning with Hezekiah and my visit to Medgar Evers's home, it's all I can do to stand.

My journey had worn me down, an embarrassing claim when contrasted with the 1961 Freedom Rides, in which every moment of every mile held the potential for violence. My exhaustion emerged not from any threat I had felt but because of the hard truths I had faced. Chief among them was confirmation of William Faulkner's observation that "the past is never dead. It's not even past."

The Freedom Riders are proof of this. We needn't go back to 1961 to confront our nation's racial problems. Instead we only have to recite the names of more recent victims of violence: Eric Garner, Michael Brown, Alton Sterling, and numerous others. This is not meant to be a repudiation of law enforcement, just an acknowledgment of the continued struggles and of the fact that despite our efforts to forming a "more perfect union," there's no clear blueprint to get us there.

What the Freedom Riders have taught us—or, at least, taught me—is that individual acts of heroism can go a long way in building that blueprint. The Freedom Riders are but one example of individuals willing to risk their lives for a common cause, and in my opinion they're one of the best examples— not only because of the effectiveness of their direct action protest but also because of the grace with which they carried it out. They were guaranteed nothing, not even safety; nonetheless, they still boarded buses and violated customs in an attempt to shape the world they wanted.

By this point in my trip I had seen about as much of our world as I could handle. So when I saw the dome of Jackson's Russell C. Davis Planetarium later that afternoon, I took the opportunity to vacate our planet for a while. I forked over five bucks and took my seat in the nearly empty auditorium. Tilting my head skyward, I waited for the show to begin. I tried to pay attention to the narrator's booming voice, but all I could think about was Hezekiah's midnight ride in the paddy wagon, Catherine Burks-Brooks's predawn chat with the Bull, Bill Harbour's letter from his mother informing him not to come home, and Jim Zwerg's prayer for the mob's salvation. I thought of Charles Person asking my students and me, "What would you get on the bus for?" And of course I thought of Bernard LaFayette belting out freedom songs, Mimi Feingold hunkered low while being driven through the streets of Montgomery, and Susan Wilbur covering her head as best she could while being pelted with a pocketbook.

Inside that dark theater the combination of the air-conditioning and the narrator's voice was enough to put me to sleep. It was a glorious sleep, and I dreamed that I was back home. When I awoke sometime later, all I saw above me were stars. They were beautiful and they were everywhere, and I imagined what they might look like from behind the bars at Parchman Farm. I rubbed my eyes, regained my bearings, and listened as a ubiquitous voice boomed over the loudspeakers. "Let us take comfort in the stability of our own world," the narrator says.

What stability? I wondered.

9

Arione Irby

Gee's Bend, Alabama

"You know, people always ask me why in the world I still live in Alabama, why I'd ever want to go back to Alabama. But this is home for me. And you cannot run from reality, you have to face it."

My ride couldn't end without a visit to the Alabama State Capitol, and so in late May 2016 I parked my car in the shadow of the rotunda, then passed through the metal detector. "Excuse me," I said to the guard, "do you know where I can find Mr. Irby?"

"Oh sure," the guard replied, smiling, and pointed to the second floor. "I think I hear him now."

I took the stairs two at a time, and soon I heard him, too. On the second floor stood seventy-year-old Arione Irby, the capitol's beloved tour guide, who after twelve years of leading tours seemed to know every inch of the place and every story about it. And there are indeed many stories to know.

Built in 1851 by slave labor, the Alabama State Capitol maintains a long and complicated history. Not only did the building briefly serve as the capitol for the Confederate States of America, its grounds also hosted the inauguration of the Confederacy's president, Jefferson Davis. Today a brass star commemorates the exact location where Davis took his oath; it's the same location where Governor George Wallace took his own oath just over a hundred years later, using the backdrop to declare the infamous line for which he's most remembered: "Segregation now, segregation tomorrow, and segregation forever."

Throughout the capitol's 165-year history, governors and legislators have regularly done battle with the federal government and occasionally even spied on their own citizens—most notably through the formation of the Alabama

Figure 10. Arione Irby, 2015.

Used by permission of Jodi Thesing-Ritter.

Sovereignty Commission in 1963, an organization (much like Mississippi's Sovereignty Commission) committed to "safe-guarding the rights of the state from the encroachment by any agency of the federal government." The secession vote passed within its walls, as did Jim Crow laws and, in between, nearly a century's worth of legislation, some of which aligned with the state's prowhite agenda. On the evening of May 19, 1961, the state capitol was again the site of a history-making moment: Governor John Patterson begrudgingly shared a table with John Seigenthaler, the assistant to the assistant attorney general, as the latter attempted to persuade the former to provide protection for the Freedom Riders during their brief stint in the state.

"Now let's head over this way," Irby called, leading the tour group toward the hall of governors. "I want to introduce you to our state's only female governor." (We were still about a year away from the April 2017 inauguration of Alabama's second female governor.) The group had just reached the marble bust of Lurleen Wallace when Irby noticed that I'd infiltrated his tour. "Well hey," he said, offering me a wide grin. "You're early." Guilty as charged.

Ever since first being on Ibry's tour a few months earlier, during our university's civil rights pilgrimage, I had been anxious for an encore performance. Though no Freedom Rider, Irby had firsthand knowledge of the state and its history, which made him the perfect person to speak with—a witness to everything, an observer to all. He is the perfect person to listen to, and I had even arranged to meet him for lunch after the tour. Irby gave me a quick pat on the back before returning his attention to the tour group.

"Now then, as I was saying," he continued, guiding us forward, "we are now inside the main entrance. This capitol goes from civil war to civil rights with 104 years in between. And right out the window there is one of the most historically important streets in America. Why don't y'all take a minute to look out?"

We did, and what we saw, past the pillars, was Dexter Avenue in all its glory. To our left sat the Dexter Avenue King Memorial Baptist Church, and not far beyond it was the First White House of the Confederacy. Meanwhile, directly ahead was the street itself, where on March 25, 1965, at the conclusion of the march from Selma to Montgomery, Dr. King spoke to a crowd of twenty-five thousand. Finally, farther down and just beyond view, was the Greyhound station itself, where on May 20, 1961, the Freedom Riders were beaten.

This is but a fraction of the history that occurred in Montgomery, a city simultaneously known as the "cradle of the Confederacy" and the birthplace of Alabama's modern civil rights movement. It's an ironic pairing, although perhaps it is causal, too. After all, when a man like Governor Wallace fights to defend "segregation forever," a man like Dr. King must rise up to combat it. Circumstances often linked the pair while both men were alive, and even after Dr. King's death their legacies continued to overlap.

"I was a member of Dexter for four years when I was at Alabama State University," Irby told the tour group as we peered at the church. "I was in the church the night Governor George C. Wallace apologized. And I'm here to tell you that he did have a change of heart."

"Mm-hmm—sure did," the others echoed. But I was skeptical. Although many Alabamians agree with Irby's assessment, I've always been troubled by the timing of Wallace's so-called redemption. After years of enacting policies detrimental to black people, the wheelchair-bound Wallace had decided to make peace with the very constituency that proved vital to his reelection. Not only that, but he chose Dr. King's former church as his backdrop. "He apologized in tears for seven minutes," Irby described. "In fact, Governor George C. Wallace probably ended up doing more for the state of Alabama—some of it accidentally—than the rest of the governors put together." I raised an eyebrow skeptically, eager to follow up at the appropriate time.

As the tour wound down, an elderly woman raised her hand and started in on a tirade about one of the political parties. I felt the tension rise in the room, and my eyes turned to Irby, who listened respectfully without providing so much as a clue to his own thoughts on the matter. After listing her grievances, the woman turned her attention to Irby and asked, "Well? How do *you* feel about that?"

"You know, my position with the state of Alabama, as a historian, I can't comment on that inside this building," Irby replied tactfully. "I can't say a word politically inside this building. But I'm glad to listen to you! You can say anything you want to. And when I get out of this building, I can say whatever I want to." The answer hardly satisfied the woman, but it satisfied me. It was, in fact, the perfectly political answer to avoiding the question of politics.

Five minutes later, at the tour's conclusion, Irby and I headed toward the doors. "Come on," he said, "let's get out of this building."

═══

We arrived at Dreamland Bar-B-Que ten minutes later and sat down at a table near the back. Even before the sweet tea arrived, Irby started on his story. "I'm from Gee's Bend way down in the bend," he began, "about ninety miles west of here. Now, growing up there, there wasn't much transportation. We had wagons and mules, and we were always walking. Thankfully, the houses were close together."

It was these walks, he explained, that strengthened the community—especially the Sunday morning walks to and from church. One particular Sunday morning, however, when he was about nine, the centerpiece of the community was destroyed. Dressed in their Sunday best, young Arione, his parents, and his fourteen siblings had just rounded the corner toward Oak Grove Baptist Church when the Irby family spotted a group of hooded Klansmen setting the place on fire.

The family stood in shocked silence, and eventually the hooded men turned around and noticed them. "If you say anything," one of the hooded men growled, "we'll do you the same way."

"So what'd you do?" I asked.

"We just watched."

"They burned your church before your eyes?"

He nodded. "You have to understand," Irby reminded me, "that these types of things happened all the time." In addition to the church burning, there were several instances throughout his childhood when young white men tore through his neighborhood blasting bullets into people's windows. "And who are you going to report it to?" he asked rhetorically. Like many small southern towns at the time, Gee's Bend had a lackluster police force whose white officers were rarely interested in investigating crimes committed against black people. Of course, systemic problems of race extended well beyond local law enforcement, Irby explained. The real problem, he said, involved repressing the black vote.

Irby told me that during election season the town often closed both County Road 29 and the ferry, making it all but impossible for the citizens of Gee's Bend, a majority black community, to travel the thirty-six miles to Camden to register to vote. Blacks could *technically* register, of course, but they had better be prepared to walk. These barriers often achieved their purpose: to dramatically limit the black vote and all but ensure the continuation of a prowhite political agenda, from law enforcement to education. As a result, self-reliance became the weapon of choice of the black community—one of the few it had at its disposal. "My father was big on this," Irby said. "He told us this every day of our lives. He said, 'Just take what you have and make what you need.' And it works, even today."

Take what you have and make what you need. It's a line seemingly drawn directly from the Freedom Riders' playbook. Although they often didn't have much—including local support, federal support, or even regular access to hospitals and taxis—they nevertheless made use of the resources at their disposal. Most notably these were courage, creativity, and a moral high ground that emboldened them further. In their more hopeful moments some Riders believed themselves invincible, their mission unstoppable, and their ultimate success a foregone conclusion. At the time it was precisely what their cause required: confirmation that through their good works they were improving the world—no matter what the cost.

"I've been the victim of terrorism all my life," Irby told me, "watching people die together, get hurt together, just like the Freedom Riders. We have got to educate ourselves. My father was big on education. He didn't have much himself, but he always told us the key to success was education. That's what I believe today."

I nodded, my mind drifting to Governor Wallace's Stand in the School-house Door. As I considered Wallace's obstructionist efforts, I recalled the eyebrow-raising comment I'd heard Irby offer previously. "Earlier today," I reminded him, "you told your tour that Governor Wallace did more for the state of Alabama than all the other governors combined—even if some of it was accidental. What'd you mean by that?"

Irby smiled and leaned in close. "You always need an agitator," he said. My clueless look compelled him to explain. "It's like when you clean your clothes in the washer," he clarified. "If you don't add the agitator, the detergent, then your clothes won't ever get clean."

I smiled as I began to catch on. "So through Wallace's stands, his acts of bigotry, he actually helped inspire the movement?"

"Oh, he did," Irby affirmed without hesitation. "He sure did."

═══

My stomach was full and my mind was reeling as Irby drove me back to my car. There was so much to take in, so much to reconsider. For instance, even though my journey would soon come to its close, it was also just beginning. We headed north up Columbus Street and turned right onto North Bainbridge Street. We passed streets that were familiar to him and foreign to me, and eventually the capitol's rotunda came into view: a beautiful symbol of an often-tense history of the state.

Yet rather than turn his back on the state or even leave it altogether, Irby had always become even more involved. He could often be found *inside* the state capitol, whereas at the start of his life he couldn't even walk through its front door. "I want you to leave here knowing that we have come a long way," he stated, "but the opportunity is here now to do much more. And," he added, looking me straight in the eye, "we're throwing it away."

I was taken aback by this last part as Irby, a fount of eternal optimism and good humor, suddenly turned glum. Like so many of his fellow civil rights foot soldiers, he feared that his generation had failed to pass the story on to the next generation. "You'll hear from a lot of us who, at the time, were not thinking of tomorrow. We were too busy getting through the day. So we just moved right on through."

In the process, many of the individual pieces of the civil rights story were lost, and as a result, Irby feared, the younger generation failed to become inspired by its predecessors. Although civil rights demonstrators such as the Freedom Riders helped to dismantle segregation, they also lived a narrative that had the potential to inspire generations to come. Yet it didn't, Irby said.

"I'll tell you what," he continued, putting his truck in park alongside my rental car. "I'm just elated that you'd think enough of me to reach out to me for your project. I appreciate more than anything else you trying to pick up the pieces and put them in letter form so more people can read it."

"It's nothing," I explained. "Really. You lived it, you *are* the story. All I do is write about it."

"That's not nothing," he emphasized. "And it's important that it's coming from a guy like you, from a white man. Because it's further proof that y'all ain't bad." He laughed. "That it matters to all of us."

I nodded.

"You know," he said, staring out at the capitol, "people always ask me why in the world I still live in Alabama, why I'd ever want to go back to Alabama. But this is home for me. And you cannot run from reality, you have to face it."

"Thanks, Mr. Irby," I said. "I'll remember that."

He shook my hand. "You keep in touch now," he called. "You hear?"

I waved as he drove off, leaving me in the shadow of the state capitol. Indeed, it has a heavy history, but it is American history, with which we are entwined, which ensnares us and weaves us together. I didn't get in my car. I didn't drive away. Instead I stood there and faced it.

Epilogue

The Last Stop

On a Friday morning in September 2015, nearly eight months before I hit the road, I settled down at a wooden table in our university's archive and began leafing through an interlibrary-loan box of CORE records. My eyes scanned countless personal notes and memoranda and eventually landed on a folder overflowing with a pile of blue papers. I opened it and was surprised to find a selection of original Freedom Rider applications. For a moment I could not believe what I had found.

The application form was a model of simplicity. Taking up no more than three-quarters of a page, it began with a basic agreement describing the project and its potential danger: "I wish to apply for acceptance as a participant in CORE's Freedom Ride 1961 to travel via bus from Washington, DC, to New Orleans, Louisiana and to test and challenge segregated facilities enroute. I understand that I shall be participating in a nonviolent protest against racial discrimination, that arrest or personal injury to me might result, and that, by signing this application, I waive all rights to damage against CORE—the Congress of Racial Equality, its directors, its officers, any other sponsoring organization, and all others in any way connected with Freedom Ride."

Directly beneath that were spaces for two signatures: the applicant's and, for applicants under the age of twenty-one, a parent's or guardian's. Most of what followed were details about the applicant's basic biographical information: name, age, sex, race, address, phone, and college or place of occupation. Then there were a few lines for listing references, and the final question inquired about the applicant's "past experience with nonviolent action." This, I knew, was the most important question of all: confirmation to James

Farmer and the rest of CORE's inner circle that the applicant could take a punch without returning one.

I flipped through several applications, scanning the names at the top (e.g., Mae Francis Moultrie, Herman Harris, B. Elton Cox) until I came to John Lewis. Lewis later became the chairman of SNCC and has served as a congressman for Georgia's Fifth District since 1987. But on that spring day in 1961, when he sat down to fill out his Freedom Riders application, his future remained unclear—even if his resolve wasn't.

"I am a student at American Baptist Theological Seminary," he wrote. "I hope to graduate in June, but on the [other] hand Freedom Ride is much more of [a] challenge to what I believe than a degree. I know that an education is important and I hope to get one, but at this time, human dignity is the most important thing in my life. This is the most important decision in my whole life, to decide to give up all, if necessary, for Freedom Ride, that justice and freedom might come to the Deep South." This is what was written by a twenty-one-year-old man whose personal history would become a significant part of American history, a man who would dedicate his life to fighting for the very causes he had noted in his application all those years ago.

I returned the application to the folder, wondering whether I, at age twenty-one, would have had the courage to write the same.

=====

Although displays of courage in the civil rights movement were hardly rare, they were also beside the point. For the Freedom Riders, the cause was never about the individual, but rather the success of the collective. Yet through this book I have set out to honor individuals as well—and not just those who rode the buses. Although I initially set out to write a book about the Freedom Riders, I soon learned that it was impossible to do so without mentioning many other civil rights icons: Emmett Till, Medgar Evers, Addie Mae Collins, Cynthia Wesley, Carole Robertson, and Carole Denise McNair, to name just a few. I realized that each strand of America's civil rights story is part of a larger tapestry, and to remove one strand is to weaken that fabric. This is not to say that all civil rights stories are accounted for here—far from it. Rather, I simply hope to acknowledge that history hardly occurs in a vacuum, and when we focus on one moment, we often lose sight of the circumstances surrounding it. After all, the Freedom Rides did not spring forth from nothing. The idea was inspired by those who had come before, and it would inspire many who came after. The impact of the Freedom Rides has been felt long beyond the summer of 1961. Although their impact was indeed the result of individuals called to action, the Riders' most lasting contribution was what they achieved together. They had to fill every bus seat and every jail cell, so that's what they did.

━━

If the primary goal of the Freedom Rides was to challenge the nonenforcement of the *Morgan* and *Boynton* decisions, then they undoubtedly achieved their goal. Through their efforts, the country—including the federal government, politicians, the judiciary, and citizens themselves—now had proof that law enforcement officers throughout the South were not living up to their duties. As a result of the Freedom Rides, the blind-eye era was over; no longer could these oversights be ignored.

At the behest of Attorney General Robert Kennedy, throughout the latter half of 1961 the Interstate Commerce Commission (ICC) began to take a closer look at its policies. Although in 1955 the ICC had ruled against the principle of "separate but equal" in interstate travel, the Freedom Riders had made it abundantly clear that six years later, enforcement was lackluster at best. By September 1961 they had clarified their position, and two months later the notorious white-only and colored-only signs were at last removed from bus terminals throughout the South.

The signs' removal, while pragmatic, was also symbolic. It was a new day in the South, and the Freedom Riders had helped to ensure that it was destined to be a better day. But in addition to the legal changes, a cultural shift had been signaled by the Freedom Riders' efforts as well, most notably within the civil rights movement itself.

"The Freedom Rides," wrote Raymond Arsenault, "had compounded and accelerated the changes initiated by the 1960 sit-ins, and the reconfigured world of civil rights activism—in which students generally took the lead while lawyers, ministers, and other elders struggled to keep up—looked radically different from the late-1950s movement led by the NAACP and SCLC."

It's hard to say whether the torch was passed or if it was taken; regardless, the result was the same. By 1960 it was clear that youth was now driving the civil rights movement: the madness of youth, the naïveté of youth, and the bravery of youth. Young people viewed themselves as the primary stakeholders; they were fighting for *their* future, after all. It was a charge they readily accepted, and, in fact, a charge they had already begun to adopt in the year before the Freedom Rides. As a result, the Riders brought us one step closer to our continued journey to the Beloved Community: a vision for the world in which love overcomes hate, peacefulness overcomes conflict, and our very humanness overcomes the desire to dehumanize others. First developed by American philosopher Josiah Royce, the philosophy of the Beloved Community was popularized by Dr. King, who spoke of it often. It was an aspirational end point for a journey that seemed endless.

Every day, after all, there is still a bus to be boarded, an injustice to be faced, a wrong to be set right. Yet too often we watch the bus pass us by. *What would you get on the bus for?* Charles Person asked, and my answer changes daily. Perhaps my answer is in continual flux because the world's problems are, too. Just when I set my sights on one answer, I grow distracted by another possibility. Maybe the answer to Charles's question is a simple one, and a universal one at that.

Maybe we don't board a bus to solve a problem. Maybe we board a bus for the same reason we always do: to reach a destination. And maybe our destination is, and always has been, the Beloved Community. None of us knows the exact route or the challenges we'll face in getting there. But neither of these uncertainties stopped the Freedom Riders.

Who among us today will fill the seats and lead the way to the Beloved Community? The ride will roll on, with or without us. It's time to take our seat.

Sources

This account was written from various sources, including firsthand accounts, scholarly research, and online and newspaper articles. What follows is a list of the sources I most heavily relied upon while crafting individual chapters. The sources are listed in approximate chronological order according to the information's placement within each chapter. If a source was employed multiple times throughout a chapter, I listed it only upon its initial use. The full citations are found in the bibliography that follows.

Prologue: All Aboard

The prologue was written with support of the following sources: Arsenault, *Freedom Riders*; Halberstam, *Children*; CORE Records, Wisconsin Historical Society; Roberts and Klibanoff, *Race Beat*; Peck, *Freedom Ride*; Catsam, *Freedom's Main Line*; Farmer, *Lay Bare the Heart*; D'Karlos Craig interview, March 18–27, 2016; Attenborough, *Gandhi*.

Chapter 1: James Zwerg

Chapter 1 was written with support of the following sources: James Zwerg interview, July 9, 2015; King, *Stride toward Freedom*; Branch, *Parting the Waters*; Arsenault, *Freedom Riders*; Halberstam, *Children*; John Seigenthaler, Civil Rights Oral History Project interview, June 11, 2003; Branch, *King Years*; YouTube, "FR Project"; Robert F. Kennedy Papers; Paul Savides interview, January 18, 2016. The photographs of Jim Zwerg after he was beaten and bloodied by an angry mob, as well as the photograph of the semiconscious Zwerg in the hospital, are viewable at: http://www.cnn.com/2011/US/05/16/Zwerg.freedom.rides/index.html.

Chapter 2: Susan Wilbur

Chapter 2 was written with support of the following sources: Susan Wilbur interview, October 18, 2015; Halberstam, *Children*; Houston, *Nashville Way*; Kreyling, *Classical Nashville*; James Zwerg interview, July 9, 2015; Salynn McCollum, Civil Rights Oral History Project interview, March 27, 2004; Arsenault, *Freedom Riders*; John Seigenthaler, Civil Rights Oral History Project interview, June 11, 2003; Smith, "World's Most Famous."

Chapter 3: Miriam Feingold

Chapter 3 was written with support of the following sources: Miriam (Feingold) Real interview, August 29, 2015; Farmer, *Lay Bare the Heart*; Peck, *Freedom Ride*; Reddie, *Martin Luther King*; Arsenault, *Freedom Riders*; Krieger, "Rise and Fall"; Oshinsky, *Worse Than Slavery*; Taylor and Fletcher, "Profits from Convict Labor"; Hamilton, *Trials*; Nelson, "Freedom Riders"; CORE Records, Wisconsin Historical Society; Etheridge, *Breach of Peace*.

Chapter 4: Charles Person

Chapter 4 was written with support of the following sources: Arsenault, *Freedom Riders*; Charles Person interview, March 20, 2016; D'Karlos Craig interview, March 18–27, 2016; Henry Thomas, Civil Rights Oral History Project interview, February 10, 2006; Lee, "Single Act"; "Trouble in Alabama," *Time*; Booker, "Jet Team"; Peck, *Freedom Ride*; John Seigenthaler, Civil Rights Oral History Project interview, June 11, 2003; Halberstam, *Children*.

Chapter 5: Bernard LaFayette Jr.

Chapter 5 was written with support of the following sources: Bernard LaFayette Jr. interview, May 20, 2016; LaFayette Jr. and Johnson, *Peace and Freedom*; Stanford University, Lafayette Jr. entry in *King Encyclopedia*; Halberstam, *Children*; Dorothy Walker interview, May 20, 2016; Messman, "They Refused"; Biography, "Emmett Till"; Perez-Pena, "Woman"; Krieger, "Siege"; Lewis, *Walking with the Wind*; Arsenault, *Freedom Riders*; "The South," *Time*; Valda Montgomery interview, May 22, 2016; Montgomery, *Just a Neighbor*.

Chapter 6: Bill Harbour

Chapter 6 was written with support of the following sources: Arsenault, *Freedom Riders*; Lewis, *Walking with the Wind*; Bill Harbour interview, May 21, 2016; Bill Harbour, Civil Rights Oral History Project interview, August 19, 2004; Pete Conroy interview, May 25, 2016; Freedom Riders Park, "Background"; Seyram Selase interview, May 25, 2016.

Chapter 7: Catherine Burks

Chapter 7 was written with support of the following sources: "Birmingham," *Life*; Branch, *Parting the Waters*; Cohen, "Speech That Shocked"; Catherine Burks-Brooks, Civil Rights Oral History Project interview, April 29, 1996; Catherine Burks-Brooks interview, May 25, 2016; James Comey, speech; Garrow, *FBI*; Brownlee, "Civil Disobedience"; Arsenault, *Freedom Riders*; Niven, *Politics of Injustice*; John Fox interview, April 7, 2016.

Chapter 8: Hezekiah Watkins

Chapter 8 was written with support of the following sources: Jerry Mitchell interview, May 26, 2016; Rowe-Sims, "Mississippi State"; Hezekiah Watkins interview, May 28,

2016; Biography, "James Bevel"; CORE Records, Wisconsin Historical Society; Minnie Watson interview, May 28, 2016; Perkins, "Justice Denied."

Chapter 9: Arione Irby

Chapter 9 was written with support of the following sources: Alabama Department of Archives and History, "Capitals"; Gray, "Alabama Sovereignty Commission"; Arsenault, *Freedom Riders*; Arione Irby interview, May 22, 2016; Jeffries, "Modern Civil Rights Movement."

Epilogue: The Last Stop

The epilogue was written with support of the following sources: CORE Records, Wisconsin Historical Society; Arsenault, *Freedom Riders*; Parker, "Josiah Royce."

Bibliography

Archival Research

Birmingham Civil Rights Institute. Oral History Project Collection. Birmingham, AL.

Civil Rights Digital Library. University of Georgia, Athens.

Congress of Racial Equality Records, 1941–1967. Mss. 14. Wisconsin Historical Society, Madison.

Miriam Feingold Papers, 1960–1967. Mss. 859. Wisconsin Historical Society, Madison.

Robert F. Kennedy Papers. Attorney General Papers. Box 25. Civil Rights: Alabama—May 1961, 5/15/61–5/20/61. John F. Kennedy Presidential Library, Boston.

Sovereignty Commission Online. Mississippi Department of Archives and History. http://www.mdah.ms.gov/arrec/digital_archives/sovcom/.

Jim Zwerg Papers. Beloit College Archives, Beloit, WI.

Articles and Book Chapters

"Birmingham: An Alabaman's Great Speech Lays the Blame." *Life*, September 27, 1963, 44.

Bleiberg, Larry. "Remembering the Freedom Rides 50 Years Later." *Los Angeles Times*, April 24, 2011. http://articles.latimes.com/2011/apr/24/travel/la-tr-freedomriders-20110424.

"Bloody Violence Wracks Montgomery; U.S. Rushes Agents into Alabama," *Anniston Star*, May 21, 1961, 1.

Booker, Simeon. "Jet Team Braves Mob Action." *Jet*, June 1, 1961, 14–21.

"Case against Police Opens in Montgomery." *Birmingham News*, May 29, 1961, 1.

Cohen, Andrew. "The Speech That Shocked Birmingham the Day after the Church Bombing." *Atlantic*, September 13, 2013. https://www.theatlantic.com/national/archive/2013/09/the-speech-that-shocked-birmingham-the-day-after-the-church-bombing/279565/.

"CORE Denies 'Riders' Meant to Injure U.S." *Birmingham News*, May 29, 1961, 8.

Duke, Bob. "2 Mob Victims Ready to Die for Integration." In *Reporting Civil Rights*. Vol. 1. *American Journalism, 1941–1963*, edited by Library of Congress, 585–88. New York: Library of America, 2003.

"Four Freedom Riders." *Time*, June 2, 1961, 17.

Free, James. "'Riders Overplay Hand in Capital." *Birmingham News*, May 26, 1961, 1.

———. "U.S. Withdraws Most of Marshals." *Birmingham News*, May 25, 1961, 1.

"Freedom Rider Hank Thomas Seeks Racial Reconciliation after 50 Years of Change."

Jackson Advocate, March 17, 2011. http://www.jacksonadvocateonline.com/ freedom-rider-hank-thomas-seeks-racial-reconciliation-after-50-years-of-change/.

"Freedom Riders against Reason." *Birmingham News*, May 25, 1961, 2.

Garrow, David. "The FBI and Martin Luther King." *Atlantic*, July–August 2002. https:// www.theatlantic.com/magazine/archive/2002/07/the-fbi-and-martin-luther-king/ 302537/.

Holloway, Frank. "Travel Notes from a Deep South Tourist." In *Reporting Civil Rights*. Vol. 1, *American Journalism, 1941–1963*, edited by Library of Congress, 595–606. New York: Library of America, 2003.

Hughes, Bettye Rice. "A Negro Tourist in Dixie." In *Reporting Civil Rights*. Vol. 1, *American Journalism, 1941–1963*, edited by Library of Congress, 633–38 . New York: Library of America, 2003.

Krieger, Daniel. "The Siege of the Freedom Riders." *New York Times*, May 19, 2011. http://www.nytimes.com/2011/05/20/opinion/20Lafayette.html.

Loory, Stuart H. "Reporter Tails 'Freedom' Bus Caught in Riot." In *Reporting Civil Rights*. Vol. 1, *American Journalism, 1941–1963*, edited by Library of Congress, 573–79. New York: Library of America, 2003.

Messman, Terry. "They Refused to Let Justice Be Crucified. *Street Spirit*. July 11, 2014. http://www.thestreetspirit.org/they-refused-to-let-justice-be-crucified-on-the-streets-of-selma/.

Perkins, Ken Parrish. "Justice Denied." *Chicago Tribune*, July 11, 1994. http://articles. chicagotribune.com/1994–07–11/features/9407110047_1_field-secretary-myrlie-evers-southern-justice.

Perez-Pena, Richard. "Woman Linked to 1955 Emmett Till Murder Tells Historian Her Claims Were False." *New York Times*, January 27, 2017. https://www.nytimes. com/2017/01/27/us/emmett-till-lynching-carolyn-bryant-donham.html?_r=0

Pullen, Crary. "Freedom Riders: Bruce Davidson on His Awakening." *Time*, May 24, 2011. http://time.com/3777390/freedom-riders-bruce-davidson-on-his-awakening/

"The South and the Freedom Riders: Crisis in Civil Rights." *Time*, June 2, 1961, 14–18.

Taylor, W. B., and T. H. Fletcher. "Profits from Convict Labor: Reality or Myth Observations in Mississippi: 1907–1934. *Journal of Police and Criminal Psychology*, 5.1, March 1989. 30–38. https://link.springer.com/article/10.1007%2FBF02809207.

"Trouble in Alabama." *Time*, May 26, 1961, 16–17.

Turner, Nathan Jr. "Birmingham Freedom Rider Catherine Brooks Recalls Perilous Journey for Justice." *Birmingham News*, April 24, 2011. http://blog.al.com/spot-news/2011/04/birmingham_freedom_rider_cathe.html

Watson, Dylan. "Hezekiah Watkins." *Jackson Free Press*, January 17, 2011. http://www. jacksonfreepress.com/news/2011/jan/17/hezekiah-watkins/.

"World Press Views Freedom Rides and the United States." *New South*, July–August 1961, 11–15.

Audio

Arsenault, Raymond. "Get on the Bus: The Freedom Riders of 1961." Interview by Terry Gross. *Fresh Air.* National Public Radio, January 12, 2006.

Books

Armstrong, Thomas, and Natalie Bell. *Autobiography of a Freedom Rider.* Deerfield Beach, FL: Health Communications, 2011.

Arsenault, Raymond. *Freedom Riders: 1961 and the Struggle for Racial Justice.* New York: Oxford University Press, 2006.

Bausum, Ann. *Freedom Riders: John Lewis and Jim Zwerg on the Front Lines of the Civil Rights Movement.* Wash., DC: National Geographic Children's Books, 2006.

Branch, Taylor. *At Canaan's Edge: America in the King Years, 1965–68.* New York: Simon & Schuster, 2006.

———. *The King Years: Historic Moments in the Civil Rights Movement.* New York: Simon & Schuster, 2013.

———. *Parting the Waters: America in the King Years, 1954–63.* New York: Simon & Schuster, 1989.

———. *Pillar of Fire: America in the King Years, 1963–65.* New York: Simon & Schuster, 1999.

Cash, W. J. *The Mind of the South.* New York: Vintage Books, 1991.

Catsam, Derek. *Freedom's Main Line: The Journey of Reconciliation and the Freedom Rides.* Lexington: University Press of Kentucky, 2009.

Eskew, Glenn T. *But for Birmingham: The Local and National Movements in the Civil Rights Struggle.* Chapel Hill: University of North Carolina Press, 1997.

Etheridge, Eric. *Breach of Peace: Portraits of the 1961 Mississippi Freedom Riders.* New York: Atlas, 2008.

Evers, Myrlie. *For Us, the Living.* Oxford: University Press of Mississippi, 1996.

Farmer, James. *Lay Bare the Heart: An Autobiography of the Civil Rights Movement.* Fort Worth: Texas Christian University Press, 1998.

Feldman, Glenn. *Politics, Society, and the Klan in Alabama, 1915–1949.* Tuscaloosa: University of Alabama Press, 1999.

Galliard, Frye. *Alabama's Civil Rights Trail: An Illustrated Guide to the Cradle of Freedom.* Tuscaloosa: University of Alabama Press, 2010.

———. *Cradle of Freedom: Alabama and the Movement That Changed America.* Tuscaloosa: University of Alabama Press, 2006.

Garrow, David J. *Birmingham, Alabama, 1956–1963: The Black Struggle for Civil Rights.* New York: Carlson, 1989.

Graetz, Robert S. *A White Preacher's Message on Race and Reconciliation: Based on His Experiences Beginning with the Montgomery Bus Boycott.* Montgomery, AL: New South Books, 2011.

Greenhaw, Wayne. *Fighting the Devil in Dixie: How Civil Rights Activists Took on the Ku Klux Klan in Alabama*. Chicago: Lawrence Hills Books, 2011.

Halberstam David. *The Children*. New York: Fawcett Books, 1999.

Hamilton, Mary Mann. *Trials of the Earth: The True Story of a Pioneer Woman*. New York: Little, Brown and Company, 2016.

Houston, Benjamin. *The Nashville Way: Racial Etiquette and the Struggle for Social Justice in a Southern City*. Athens: University of Georgia Press, 2012.

King, Martin Luther. *Stride toward Freedom: The Montgomery Story*. New York: Harper, 1958.

Kreyling, Christine. *Classical Nashville: Athens of the South*. Nashville: Vanderbilt University Press, 1996.

LaFayette Jr., Bernard, and Kathryn Lee Johnson. *In Peace and Freedom: My Journey in Selma*. Lexington: University Press of Kentucky, 2013.

Lewis, John. *Walking with the Wind: A Memoir of the Movement*. New York: Simon & Schuster, 1998.

Library of Congress, ed. *Reporting Civil Rights*. Vol. 1, *American Journalism, 1941–1963*. New York: Library of America, 2003.

———. *Reporting Civil Rights*. Vol. 2, *American Journalism 1963–1973*. New York: Library of America, 2003.

McWhorter, Diane. *Carry Me Home: Birmingham, Alabama—the Climactic Battle of the Civil Rights Revolution*. New York: Touchstone, 2001.

Montgomery, Valda Harris. *Just a Neighbor: A Child's Memoir of the Civil Rights Movement*. Montgomery, AL: McQuick, 2010.

Newton, Michael. *The Ku Klux Klan*. Jefferson, NC: McFarland, 2007.

Niven, David. *The Politics of Injustice: The Kennedys, the Freedom Riders, and the Electoral Consequences of a Moral Compromise*. Knoxville: University of Tennessee Press, 2003.

Olson, Lynne. *Freedom's Daughters: The Unsung Heroines of the Civil Rights Movement from 1830 to 1970*. New York: Scribner, 2002.

Oshinsky, David M. *"Worse Than Slavery": Parchman Farm and the Ordeal of Jim Crow Justice*. New York: Free Press, 1996.

Peck, James. *Freedom Ride*. New York: Simon & Schuster, 1962.

Raines, Howell. *My Soul Is Rested: Movement Days in the Deep South*. New York: Penguin, 1983.

Reddie, Richard. *Martin Luther King, Jr: History Maker*. Oxford, UK: Lion Hudson, 2011.

Roberts, Gene, and Hank Klibanoff. *The Race Beat: The Press, the Civil Rights Struggle, and the Awakening of a Nation*. New York: Vintage Books, 2007.

Rowe, Gary Thomas. *My Undercover Years with the Ku Klux Klan*. New York: Bantam Books, 1976.

Silver, Carol Ruth. *Freedom Rider Diary*. Jackson: University Press of Mississippi, 2014.

Sims, Patsy. *The Klan*. Lexington: University Press of Kentucky, 1996.

Watson, Bruce. *Freedom Summer: The Savage Season of 1964 That Made Mississippi Burn and Made America a Democracy.* New York: Viking Press, 2010.

Zellner, Bob, and Constance Curry. *The Wrong Side of Murder Creek.* Montgomery, AL: New South Books, 2008.

Electronic Sources

Alabama Department of Archives and History. "Capitals of Alabama." http://www.archives.state.al.us/capital/capitals.html.

Biography. "Emmett Till." http://www.biography.com/people/emmett-till-507515.

———. "James Bevel." http://www.biography.com/people/james-bevel-21399887.

Brownlee, Kimberley. "Civil Disobedience." *The Stanford Encyclopedia of Philosophy,* Winter 2016. https://plato.stanford.edu/archives/win2016/entries/civil-disobedience/.

Freedom Riders Park. "Background." http://www.freedomriderspark.org/background.html.

Gray, Jeremy. "Alabama Sovereignty Commission Formed with Sweeping Powers, No Public Oversight." Alabama, October 5, 1963. http://blog.al.com/birmingham-news-stories/2013/10/alabama_sovereignty_commission.html.

Jeffries, Hassan Kwame. "Modern Civil Rights Movement in Alabama" *Encyclopedia of Alabama,* July 17, 2015. http://www.encyclopediaofalabama.org/article/h-1580.

Krieger, Daniel. "The Rise and Fall—and Rise—of 'Jewess': Why Are Twenty-First-Century Women Reclaiming a Derogatory Term?" Nextbook, May 14, 2008. http://www.danielkrieger.net/pdf/The%20Rise%20and%20Fall—and%20Rise—of%20"Jewess".pdf.

Lee, Cynthia. "A Single Act of Kindness Becomes Part of Civil Rights Lore." UCLA Newsroom, May 10, 2011. http://newsroom.ucla.edu/stories/civil-rights-activists-still-remember-203453.

Parker, Kelly A. "Josiah Royce." *The Stanford Encyclopedia of Philosophy,* Summer 2014. https://plato.stanford.edu/entries/royce/.

Rowe-Sims, Sarah. "The Mississippi State Sovereignty Commission." Mississippi History Now, September 2002. http://mshistorynow.mdah.state.ms.us/index.php?id=243.

Smith, Owen. "World's Most Famous Police Officers—Floyd Mann." NCC Home Learning, March 13, 2015. https://www.ncchomelearning.co.uk/blog/worlds-most-famous-police-officers-floyd-mann/.

Stanford University. "Lafayette, Bernard (1940–)." *King Encyclopedia.* http://kingencyclopedia.stanford.edu/encyclopedia/encyclopedia/enc_lafayette_bernard_1940.1.html.

Interviews by the Author

Burks-Brooks, Catherine. May 25, 2016

Conroy, Pete. May 25, 2016

Craig, D'Karlos. March 18–27, 2016

Fox, John. April 7, 2016
Harbour, Bill. May 21, 2016
Irby, Arione. May 22, 2016
LaFayette Jr., Bernard. May 20, 2016
Mitchell, Jerry. May 26, 2016
Montgomery, Valda. May 22, 2016
Person, Charles. March 20, 2016
Real, Miriam Feingold. August 29, 2015
Savides, Paul. January 18, 2016
Selase, Seyram. May 25, 2016
Walker, Dorothy. May 20, 2016
Watkins, Hezekiah. May 28, 2016
Watson, Minnie. May 28, 2016
Wilbur, Susan. October 18, 2015
Zwerg, James. July 9, 2015

Transcripts

Burks-Brooks, Catherine. Civil Rights Oral History Project, Special Collections Division, Nashville Public Library.

Harbour, Bill. Civil Rights Oral History Project, Special Collections Division, Nashville Public Library.

McCollum, Salynn. Civil Rights Oral History Project, Special Collections Division, Nashville Public Library.

Seigenthaler, John. Civil Rights Oral History Project, Special Collections Division, Nashville Public Library.

Thomas, Henry. Civil Rights Oral History Project, Special Collections Division, Nashville Public Library.

Speech

Comey, James. "Law Enforcement and the Communities We Serve: Tied Together in a Single Garment of Destiny." 16th Street Baptist Church, Birmingham. May 25, 2016.

Videos

Attenborough, Richard, dir. *Gandhi*. Columbia Pictures, 1982.

Bernard, Sheila, dir. "Eyes on the Prize: America's Civil Rights Movement, 1954–1985." PBS, 1987.

Nelson, Stanley, dir. "Freedom Riders." *American Experience*. PBS, 2011.

———. "Freedom Summer." *American Experience*. PBS, 2014.

YouTube. "FR Project: Jim Zwerg in Hospital." May 1, 2008.

Index